WENDY BLANDA

How to Foster a Rescue Dog

Training for you and training for your foster dog. From selecting a rescue to adoption.

Copyright © 2023 by Wendy Blanda

All rights reserved. No part of this publication may be reproduced, stored or transmitted in any form or by any means, electronic, mechanical, photocopying, recording, scanning, or otherwise without written permission from the publisher. It is illegal to copy this book, post it to a website, or distribute it by any other means without permission.

Wendy Blanda asserts the moral right to be identified as the author of this work.

Wendy Blanda has no responsibility for the persistence or accuracy of URLs for external or third-party Internet Websites referred to in this publication and does not guarantee that any content on such Websites is, or will remain, accurate or appropriate.

Designations used by companies to distinguish their products are often claimed as trademarks. All brand names and product names used in this book and on its cover are trade names, service marks, trademarks and registered trademarks of their respective owners. The publishers and the book are not associated with any product or vendor mentioned in this book. None of the companies referenced within the book have endorsed the book.

First edition

This book was professionally typeset on Reedsy.
Find out more at reedsy.com

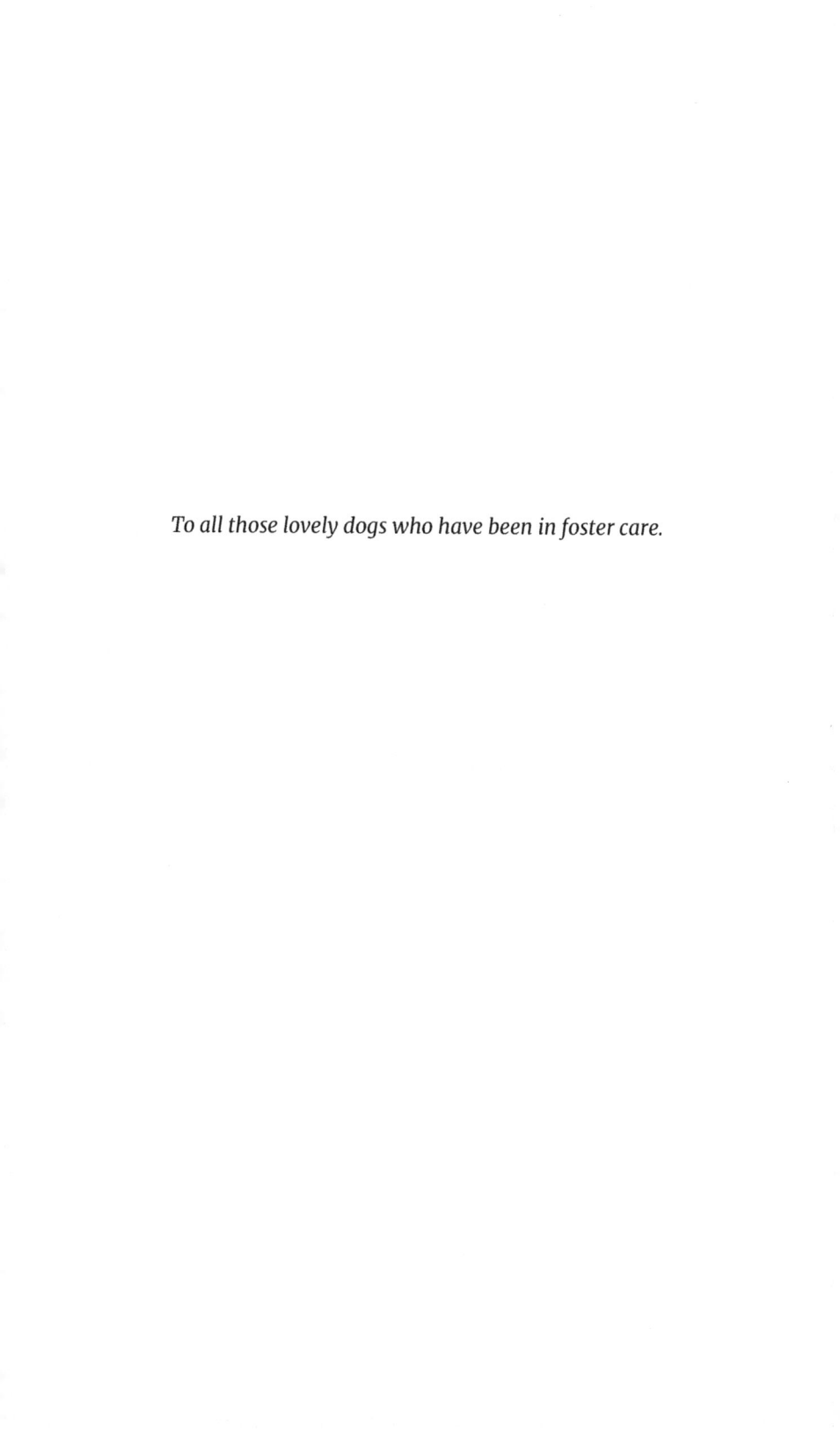

To all those lovely dogs who have been in foster care.

"The world would be a nicer place if everyone had the ability to love as unconditionally as a dog."

- M.K. Clinton

Contents

1	Introduction	1
2	The Rescue Mindset	5
3	Why Foster?	12
4	Isn't it Too Difficult to Let Them Go?	17
5	Are You Ready to Foster?	21
6	What Kind of Dog Will You Foster?	25
7	What are You Willing to Give?	32
8	Selecting a Rescue	38
9	Reaching Out	45
10	Preparing to Bring Home Your Foster	52
11	Bringing Home Your Foster	60
12	Caring for Your Foster Dog	69
13	Adoption Time	95
14	The Meet and Greet	104
15	After the Adoption	118
16	Other Ways to Volunteer	125
17	Frequently Asked Questions (FAQ's)	130
18	References and Resources	148
	Epilogue	152
	Afterword	153

1

Introduction

Hello and thank you for your interest in fostering a rescue dog. My name is Wendy Blanda and I'm extremely excited to be writing this book for you. I've fostered many dogs over the past 10 years for a few different rescue groups. I love giving a dog in need a place to land until he gets to his forever home. I've had the opportunity to get to know dogs as small as a 3 pound 59chihuahua mix named Elvie to a 90 pound pittie mix named King. Each dog has their own individual personality, needs, and journey. I consider their stay in our home to be just a stepping stone in their journey to find their people.

Personally, I have always had dogs in my life. I grew up with dogs and loved other peoples' dogs from the age of 18-25, when I got my first dog, a corgi named Einstein. I've always been the person at the party who would prefer to say hello to the dog first and could be seen sneaking out to the backyard if that's where the owner's dog was hiding out. I love to say hello to good dogs

I pass on the streets and enjoy taking my 2 dogs with me on adventures.

When I was a kid, the only homeless dogs I knew about were the ones in the local pound. Our dad brought our dog, Lady, home from there one day when I was around nine. Over the years, I first learned about greyhound rescue (for retired racing dogs), then purebred rescue, then other rescue organizations. About 20 years ago I met a group of friends who were active in dog and cat rescue, and I became intrigued, and then hooked. These friends helped me to learn about the process, giving me advice and support along the way. Now people in my life ask me about how they can get involved and I happily talk their ear off.

If you're reading this little book, then hopefully you're like I was, intrigued with the idea of volunteering to help out a rescue dog, but not sure where to begin. I'd like to help you start your journey, so that you find the same joy I've had and so that more dogs in need can be saved. In this book, I'll give you the information you need to get started. My hope for you is that by the end of this, you will have the knowledge you need to move forward and the confidence that you are capable of helping a dog to prepare for their forever home.

In this book, first I'll talk a little bit about the rescue mindset, the benefits of fostering, and about letting them go when it's time. Then I'll go through some exercises to help you decide what kind of dog you'd like to foster and what all you're willing to give. I'm a strong believer in planning! We'll go through reaching out to the rescue and preparing to bring home your canine houseguest. I'll then discuss how to care for your foster dog, including some of the challenges you might face, based

INTRODUCTION

on my personal experience. Finally, I'll discuss what to expect when your dog is ready to be adopted and their family comes to meet them. I know it doesn't stop with the adoption, though, so I'll also share a bit about what you might encounter after your foster dog leaves. I'll use "him" or "the foster" for referring to the dog, just for simplicity. In the case that, during this process, you realize that you are unable to bring a dog home, I've also added some other ways in which you can help rescue dogs in need and the rescue organizations who care for them.

Thank you for picking up this guide, for taking the time to consider fostering a rescue dog, and, hopefully, for giving a dog a place to go on a temporary basis. You can make a world of difference in the life of that dog.

If you find this book helpful, please leave a review on Amazon, pass along a copy, or post a link to the book on your rescue's website. The more help people to foster dogs, the more dogs will find loving homes. Thank you for your help.

HOW TO FOSTER A RESCUE DOG

2

The Rescue Mindset

Before talking about you and your rescue dog specifically, I'd like to help you to understand the rescue mindset. Animal rescues came about due to the pet overpopulation problem. Shelters were overcrowded and thousands of dogs were being euthanized daily. These weren't all aggressive, sickly, unadoptable dogs, these were nice dogs who would make fine pets but there just wasn't enough room to house them all. Spay and neuter wasn't very widespread (thank you, Bob Barker, for sending out the message!), and accidental litters were commonplace.

Even purebred dogs were being euthanized. Those are the people who stepped up first - those who were breeding purebred dogs, like golden retrievers, pomeranians, and dachshunds. They would see images of and hear stories of purebred dogs ending up at the local shelter. Although they had carefully selected people to care for the puppies that they had produced, some of those dogs (or their offspring) were being relinquished to the shelter. Rather than see these dogs euthanized, they started breed specific rescues. They also began implementing contracts with people who bought their puppies which were not show quality, requiring that those dogs be spayed or neutered. Good breeders stopped promoting the purchase of their puppies as a money making venture ("if you buy one female, she can return your investment with her first litter!"). Pet overpopulation changed the mindset of dog lovers.

The rescue mindset includes the idea that dogs are not a commodity. Dogs are not meant to bring in extra cash for us and should not be required to pump out litter after litter of puppies for sale. Dogs are not to be treated like investments who need to produce a monetary return or be abandoned. Dogs are companion animals. They depend on us in every way. Where once they were wolves, now they've evolved to do party tricks, sleep on our laps, and wait patiently to be fed. Good breeders only breed puppies that will go into a home for life and have a guarantee that they will take back the dog they created rather than see the dog die alone in a shelter. So, that's why the ethical breeders started to open breed-specific rescues - so that the breed that they adore does not suffer.

But not everyone adores just a specific breed. I adore all dogs (although I do have my favorites). To me, it's the personality that wins me over, not the look. Ok, I'm a sucker for big pointy ears and short legs, but I also have a soft spot for the one-of-a-kind goofball looking dogs. I'm not alone - lots of people favor the underdog. New rescues started popping up to cater to dogs that were highly adoptable, regardless of breed. This is the majority of 501c3 dog rescue nonprofit groups in the United States. Just people who love dogs and want to help them find their forever homes.

The rescue mindset also says that all dogs, regardless of breed, have value and deserve a good home. Nonprofit groups for purebreds often also include in their charter that they will pull purebred-mix dogs from shelters and find them homes, too. Many shelters now have rescue coordinators on staff who have a phone list of local purebred and mixed breed rescues, and they do their best to guess the dog breed so they can network them. It is difficult for a rescue volunteer to go to a shelter and pick up just one dog, because the shelters are typically full of good dogs looking for a chance. I've had to do it, and it's heartbreaking. All I can say to the others is "I hope you get your chance. You're a very good dog" and give them a scratch under the chin.

The rescue mindset that helps when I'm at the shelter goes

something like this, to me. I look at that one dog I'm helping and I say "A lot of dogs won't make it out of here, but you will, my friend. You are a very lucky dog." The need is endless and can be overwhelming at times. Even if I'd taken home ten dogs, there would be ten more tomorrow. You have to focus on the dog in front of you. You have to know that what you're doing is saving the life of a dog, and that matters. You can't fix everything. You have to do what is within your limits and what is sustainable in your life. I've never brought home fifty dogs, but I have done my part to save fifty dogs, one at a time.

Over the last twenty years, we've seen the pet overpopulation crisis greatly improved. The rescue mindset has spread into the community. People are spaying and neutering their pets much more often, the shelter systems are improving, legislation has moved away from treating dogs as livestock and towards humane care, and more people are adopting rather than buying a dog from a pet store. Nonprofit rescue groups have been one of the factors in this improvement. The people involved give of their time, money, and energy to help pets in need.

Rescuers do not do it for the money. The majority of people I've known have sacrificed their own money rather than let a dog in rescue go without something they need. We don't see a chihuahua at a rural shelter where the adoption fee is relatively low and think "Wow! I can flip that dog for a profit in suburbia!" For every dog whose adoption fee exceeds their individual costs, there is another who requires expensive veterinary care. Adoption fees aren't adjusted up or down based on the amount of money that dog costs the nonprofit. If that was the case, then 3-legged dogs missing half their teeth would be the most expensive dog to adopt. The rescue is responsible for the dog's healthcare while he is with the rescue, and there are often surprise vet bills.

Overall, in dog rescue, the universal objectives are to:

1. Identify dogs who have been relinquished by their owner who need help finding a home
2. Keep the dog safe during their stay with the rescue
3. Give the dogs the veterinary care they need
4. Prevent further adding to pet overpopulation by spaying and neutering each dog prior to adoption
5. Promote the rescue dog so that people will find them (on line or in person)
6. Screen potential adopters so that there is a good match

between the person and the dog
7. Help advise the new adopter on the dog's care, so that they are set up for success
8. Be a safety net for the dog in case the new home does not work out for any reason

If you resonate with the mission of dog rescue and the rescue mindset, then you are a good candidate for fostering a dog in need.

3

Why Foster?

Why foster a dog at all? There are animal shelters, there are plenty of people running 501c3 nonprofit rescues, the pet overpopulation problem isn't quite as bad as it used to be, and you have no experience. Can one person really make a difference?

Every day, people who lead rescue groups are inundated with pleas to take in dogs. The shelters call, the general public calls, texts and emails with sad faces never end. There are more dogs in need than they can take in. With one more foster, they could say no to these please just one less time. I've heard it said that fosters are like gold to a rescue. They make it possible to connect the dogs to the new owners by providing a temporary place for the dog to go while the right home is found. Without fosters, all dogs without owners would have to be housed in shelters, where there is limited space. Yes, you are needed and, yes, you make a huge difference.

There are many benefits of fostering. Of course, there is the altruistic benefit of giving back to your community. On a large scale, you'll be part of the pet overpopulation solution and a good example for your kids, family, and friends. Many people have a big heart and feel sad when they hear Sarah Mclachlan sing "in the arms of an angel..." in the Humane Society commercial. But not as many open their home to a dog in need. Feeling like you're actually making a difference is quite rewarding.

Knowing that you've helped someone connect with a good pet is also rewarding. Ever set up a friend on a date and it works out? How happy are you for your friend when they find their match and you had a hand in their connection? I get the same feeling when I have a kid in my living room trying to teach his new dog how to sit, even though they just met. I'm happy to be included in moments like these.

Another benefit of fostering is the enjoyment of having a dog in your home without the long-term commitment of having a dog for another 10-20 years. If you have a lifestyle where you're not sure if you can commit to providing a permanent home for a dog, you may want to enjoy the short-term commitment of a few weeks or months with a foster dog. While the dog is in your home, the rescue is responsible for any veterinary care that might be needed. So if the potential of vet bills have kept you from adopting a dog, then that risk is taken out of the equation.

Some people will foster a dog as a type of trial, to see what having a dog would be like. Maybe you have never had a dog before and you are unsure if it's the right decision for your family. Fostering a dog is a good way to see if owning a dog is right for you. Many foster dogs have been "foster fails", meaning that their foster home ended up being their permanent home when their foster parents decided to adopt them.

WHY FOSTER?

Case study #1 – Angela. As a young adult, Angela lives with two roommates in a rental apartment with an enclosed patio. She grew up with dogs and has always enjoyed the company of a dog. Angela works at a local coffee shop, where other dogs visit often. She would love to own a dog, her roommates love dogs, and her apartment community is dog friendly. However, she has plans to travel for most of the summer, and she's considering grad school as well. Angela is worried that the fifteen year commitment to a dog might be too much for her at this stage in her life. In a recent discussion, one of her friends suggested she get a dog, have her roommates take care of it in the summer, and then just rehome it if her life changes too much. After all, that's a better life than many dogs have! But Angela worries that it wouldn't be fair to the dog. One day, she overhears a customer ask if he can post a flier for his foster dog. Angela has a conversation with the customer about the local rescue for which he volunteers. Later on she reaches out in an email, hopeful that she can foster dogs short-term until she is ready for the long-term commitment of a dog of her own.

4

Isn't it Too Difficult to Let Them Go?

I'm not going to lie, there is always the risk that a person will cave in and adopt their foster dog. Every dog I've fostered has been a good dog, and I've treated them all like family. Every now and then I'll get teary eyed when I see an extra special dog go to their new home. It's not easy at times, especially when a friend starts pressuring me to keep the dog.

What helps is to remember the foster mindset. Although you will get all the puppy snuggles and adoring looks which melt your heart, in the end it's about that dog, not about you. You need to always be thinking about what's best for that dog, and for other shelter dogs. It's best for him or her to go to their forever home. It's best for all dogs for you to have that space open again so you can help another dog. If you're too emotionally attached to let go of this one, could you still help the next one? If the answer is yes, then, by all means, adopt a foster and keep fostering as well. I like to have two dogs of my own and keep a third space open for a foster dog. The foster benefits from interactions with my dogs, from our stable routine, and from being in a home environment instead of at the local shelter. At the end of their time here, I send them off the same way I might send my son's best friend home after a sleepover. He was never mine. He was always meant to be with them.

Where it can be difficult is when family or friends sign and say "but don't you want to keep him?" Social pressure can be rough. Instead of focusing on the sad goodbyes, I like to take a moment to tell them what I know about the dog's background. For example, I might let them know that the dog was on the euthanasia list at whatever shelter and that the rescue was able to pull him when an email plea was sent out. And now, he's here, sunning himself on the patio, and getting ready for his forever home. No, I don't want to keep him. I want to let him go and help the next dog do the same thing. Oftentimes people will tell me "I could never foster. I'd get too attached". Can they spend 40 hours a week with a good looking co-worker without falling in love with them? Can they babysit their adorable baby niece and still send her home afterwards? If they can do this, surely they could foster a dog.

What helps me, emotionally, for adoption day is to talk to the dog a lot, reinforcing that they are here for a while until they move on.
For example, I might say:

- Welcome to our home! I hope you enjoy your stay here!
- I'm going to take good care of you until your mama or daddy comes for you.
- We don't know who your people are yet, but they are out there and we'll help you find them

- You are going to make someone very happy one day
- You're such a good dog. I can't wait to meet your family.
- Guess what? Your people are coming today. They are going to keep you safe, give you good food, take you for walks, and always love you. This is the day we've been waiting for.

When that day comes, you and your foster will both be prepared for the transition.

Case study #1 (continued) - *Angela has been approved to foster! After some training and getting ready, she brings home a poodle-dachshund mix named Marcus. She feels so much happiness from having a dog at home, spending lots of time with her new friend. Her roommates, too, are excited to have Marcus around. He is a mellow dog with big button eyes who loves to cuddle while binge watching their favorite shows. Her roommates start to pressure Angela to keep Marcus. "He needs a home, and we have a home!" "He's a perfect dog!" "We will all miss him too much when he goes!" Angela is quite attached to Marcus, her little houseguest, particularly since he has been through so much in his life. Over dinner, she reminds her roommates that she is fostering to help dogs like Marcus and that she hopes she will find a perfect home for him and a few more dogs before her summer travel begins. Angela emphasizes to them that Marcus' perfect home is out there waiting for him and that all the love and care they give to him is helping him on his journey. She starts calling Marcus their "4th roommate" and joking about how it's his turn to finally unload the dishwasher. One of her roommates even suggests that they work together to foster some puppies next time.*

HOW TO FOSTER A RESCUE DOG

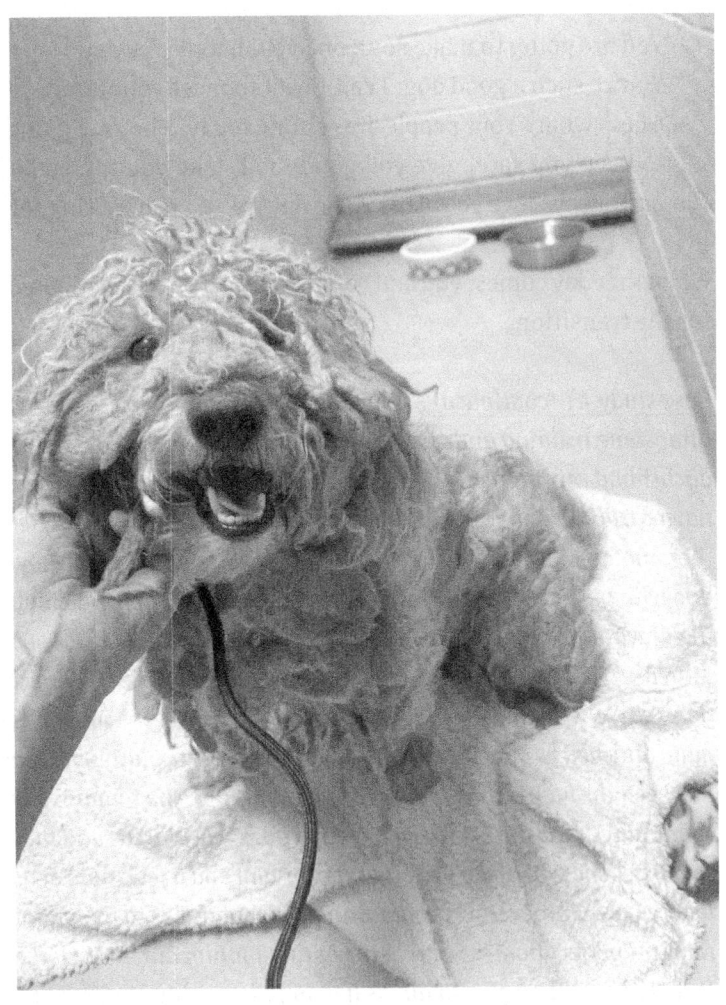

5

Are You Ready to Foster?

Fostering can be a lot like bringing home a new puppy. It takes time, preparation, patience, and cleaning skills. If you are typically gone for long hours each day, either for work or on the weekends, the foster dog could get lonely or, worse, get into trouble. Do you have time in your schedule for monitoring, training, socializing, and exercising a dog? If you live in an apartment, can you stop home at lunch to take the dog out for potty breaks? When you get home at the end of a long day, can you meet the dog's needs for playtime, socialization, and training? There is nothing like having a dog to come home to, but, as any new puppy owner will tell you, puppies can be a lot of work. Even adult dogs, in a new environment, can be a lot of work! This is not to scare you off, but to really consider the ways that having a new dog in your home can impact your routine.

Another thing to consider is how you feel about having a dog in your home at all. When you bring home a dog, you need to be ready for all that means. Do you have precious rugs which would be ruined if a dog had a potty accident? Are there valuable items in your house which could be broken by a beast who is wrestling with your resident dog? Can you secure sentimental items so that the dog cannot chew on, push over, step on, or otherwise damage? Are you ok with the potential for the financial losses in your home if you fail to fully dog proof things? Rescue organizations do not reimburse for damages in your home which are done by the dog while he is in your care. Yes, you can roll up rugs, limit the dog's access to certain rooms and encourage children to put away toys, but there's always the potential that you've overlooked something. You need to be okay with that and have the ability to expect the unexpected and roll with it if you're going to foster a rescue dog.

Finally, if you're ready to foster, then you're ready to upend your schedule, puppy proof your house and welcome in a stranger only to have them eventually leave you forever without much reward in return. Yes, you will have the love of the dog while he is there, and you will have the support and recognition of your family and friends. However, fostering a rescue dog is primarily just another way to volunteer in the community. If you already volunteer in other ways, you know it's not glamorous to sort goods at a food drive or clean up trash at the beach. But, unlike other volunteer activities, you will build a bond with this little being. If you do your job right he will happily and confidently leave you. You might form a friendship with the new owners, and you may see the dog again, but he will never be yours again (unless you are a "foster fail", which we'll get to later). Are you emotionally ready to do the hard work of bonding with and caring for a dog and then letting him be someone else's forever love? That's what's required, and it can be much more emotionally difficult than other forms of volunteerism.

If you're ready, then I guarantee you will enjoy the ride. It's fun, personally rewarding, and makes a big impact on one dog at a time. To me that's worth the three throw rugs I've pitched in the trash, the scratches dug into the cabinet that holds the treats, the Sundays at adoption events, the disgusting expulsions I've cleaned up in the middle of the night, and the emotions I've felt when the really special ones have moved on. If you're ready to foster, then a lucky rescue will welcome you with open arms.

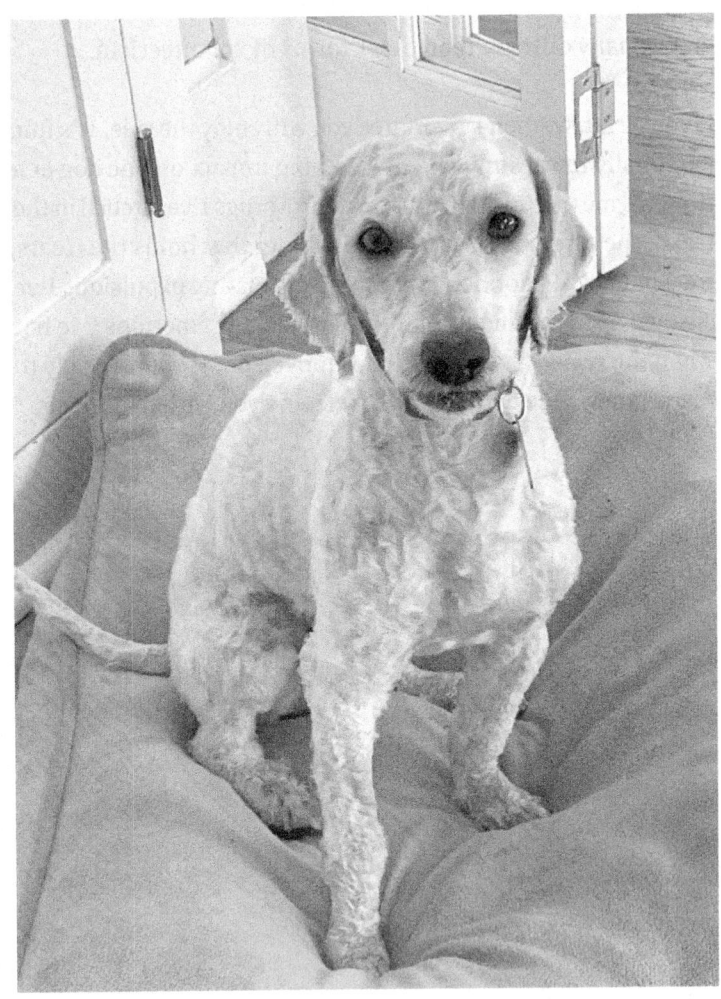

6

What Kind of Dog Will You Foster?

Before you reach out to a rescue, you should think about your own expectations. What kind of dog do you want to foster? Would you prefer a small dog or a large dog? How many dogs would you foster at once? Could you take in a pair of dogs who have been together their whole life? Could you take on a giant breed? Or a pregnant dog? Puppies? A senior dog? The need is endless, and having an idea of what you would like to do can keep you from feeling overwhelmed or from making an emotional decision under pressure.

Are you drawn to or intrigued by a type of purebred dog? Do you always want a dog within a set size range with a particular coat type? Breeds nationally recognized by the AKC have breed specific rescue organizations, found on the AKC website. In addition, there are often state-wide or local breed specific rescue organizations. Purebred rescue can have an advantage in that you have a defined size, coat type, and typical personality which are all known. You would learn what health, behavioral, and grooming needs are typical for that breed, making fostering the same breed easier with time. If you have a passion for purebred dogs, there are many rescues that are overwhelmed and could use your help.

Although within a breed there is a typical personality, not all dogs conform to the norm. There are dogs of every breed who buck the trend. If what is more important to you is personality, then a mixed breed rescue might be your choice. Mixed breed dogs come in all shapes, sizes, and personalities. Some are so far from any breed standard that people have a hard time identifying any one breed in the mix. Consider some of the traits in the table below and think about what you are accepting of for your home.

Dog Trait Considerations			
Size	<10 lbs	10-25 lbs	25-60 lbs	>60
Sex	Male		Female	
Age	0-12 weeks	3 months - 2 years	2 - 8 years	> 8 years
Exercise needs	Couch potato	Easy walks	Rigorous walks	Running partner
Coat length	Hairless	Short	Medium	Long
Shedding	Non-shedding	Minor shedding	Sheds regularly	Heavy shedding
Training needs (general)	Completely untrained	Walks nicely on leash but knows no commands	Knows some commands	Obedience pro
Training needs (potty)	Completely untrained	Needs some reinforcement / has occasional accidents	Rarely has accidents	Notifies you when needs to go outside
Vocalization	Never barks	Sometimes barks	Barks to alert owner	Barks when left alone
Medical	Already has spay/neuter, shots, and microchip	Needs medication or isolation temporarily.	Needs easy medical care long-term	High needs (Pregnant, blind, deaf, epileptic, etc.)
Socialization (dogs)	Loves other dogs	Indifferent towards other dogs	Selectively social	Must be an only dog
Socialization (people)	Unsocialized	Afraid of some people	Welcomes new people after a few minutes	Loves everyone, big and small
Socialization (cats)	Not cat friendly	Excitable, but manageable	Ok with cats within their home	Loves all cats
Number of dogs	0	1	2	Nursing mom with litter

For many rescue dogs, the information beyond their physical appearance and health evaluation is simply unknown. It will be up to you to discover if they know how to sit, potty outside, and shed profusely. But it's good to think through which qualities are must haves, which are nice to haves, and which are deal breakers. If your condo complex does not allow dogs over 15 pounds and your neighbors complain to the HOA a lot, and your spouse is allergic to dogs, then you'll want to let the rescue know that you can foster non-shedding dogs under 15 pounds who are not overly vocal. If you've shared these boundaries and the dog you have is not a good fit, then you can reach back out to the coordinator and ask if they can switch dogs with another foster.

If there are other members of your household, discuss these topics with them as well. You may be welcoming toward a hundred and eighty pound slobbering English mastiff, while your spouse or kids could be afraid of giant dogs. On the other hand, they might be excited to raise a litter of terrier puppies with you. It is much less stressful to have a partner who cleans up a puddle in the living room than one who is shocked and disgusted that the new dog isn't 100% potty trained. Agreeing on expectations will set you up for success

I recommend that first time fosters take on an easy dog. Start off asking for one nice adult dog (male or female) who is relatively calm and social. Don't take on a dog with major physical or behavioral needs as your first foster. There are plenty of easy dogs out there who will appreciate you just as much.

Case Study #2 - Rachel. Never having fostered before, Rachel has thought long and hard about what it would mean to have a foster dog in her home. She has two senior dogs who are both under fifteen pounds and already have their own routine for daily medical needs. She can't imagine bringing in a dog who would expect "the ladies" to entertain it. She also can't fathom having a large dog who could potentially step on her small dogs. Rachel loves her two girls so much and it breaks her heart whenever she sees other senior dogs in need. She would adopt them all if she could afford the medical bills! Her dogs are so easy to care for, napping in the sun, going on short walks, snuggling on the couch, and, occasionally, playing tug of war with their toy bunny. After doing some internet searching, Rachel finds a local rescue that specializes in senior dogs. She reaches out to them, letting them know about her household and that she would like to foster one dog who is around the same size as her girls. Rachel lets them know that the dog should be mellow and dog-friendly, and that she's open to any breed. She lets them know that barking doesn't bother her but that the dog should be pretty consistent with potty training. Once she is approved as a foster, Rachel brings home a twelve year old dachshund-chihuahua with a food allergy named Rocky. Since her dogs are already on a special diet, Rachel finds it easy to prepare Rocky's meals. After a bit of an initial transition, the ladies allow Rocky to share their spot in the sunbeam during afternoon naps.

7

What are You Willing to Give?

In addition to the type of dog you'd like to foster, you should also think about what you're willing to give. Besides space, there is also daily time, duration of time, money, and transportation, and medical care to consider. As mentioned earlier, the need is endless. If you bought a farm in the countryside and spent all of your time and money caring for one hundred foster dogs, there would still be more in need. To avoid volunteer burnout, straining your relationships, and financial stress, it's best to think about your limits.

First, think about the daily time commitment. Do you work full-time away from home? Would the dog be home for 8 or more hours a day? In that case, your daily time availability is mornings, evenings, and weekends. Puppies generally require more time commitment due to their feeding schedule and potty training. Do you love to run? Can you commit to long walks daily? If so, you could offer to take in a dog who has higher daily exercise commitments. Do you live at a place with no outdoor access for mid-day potty? Some dogs need a mid-day potty walk, so consider if you have time to stop home mid-day. Do you have fifteen minutes you can spend in the evening to work on some basic socialization, training, or medical care? Can you drop the dog off to be neutered or will you need a volunteer to help with transportation? If the rescue holds weekend adoption events, can you take the dog to the event location?

Next, think about the long-term commitment. Some dogs are adopted within a week. Some take three months, six months, or longer. The reasons vary - some are related to the dog's physical characteristics, some are related to the individual dog's needs, and some are related to the response time and screening process of the rescue. Be sure to ask the rescue coordinator about their expectations and relay back to them your limits. Whatever length of time that you can offer will be greatly appreciated by the dog and by any good nonprofit group.

Finally, think about the financial aspects of fostering. The dog will need food, toys, and other supplies. There is gas money associated with transit. Paying for medical supplies is the responsibility of the rescue but fosters often pay for some or all of the other supplies. The rescue will most likely offer to pay for food and provide you with a dog crate, a collar and leash, etc. It's your responsibility to let them know which supplies you need and when. Otherwise, it might be assumed that you are donating supplies to the rescue for the care of your foster dog.

The table below shows a responsibility matrix related to time and money commitments. This is just an example, based off of the rescues that I have encountered. The rescue you choose to volunteer for may have different expectations, but this table will give you some talking points so that expectations are understood on both sides.

Time and Money Responsibility Matrix Example		
Commitments	Rescue	Foster
Housing	No	Yes
Exercise	No	Yes
Basic socialization / training	No	Yes
Extensive training	If needed for special cases	No
Potty breaks	No	Yes
Basic grooming (baths, brushing, nails, etc.)	No	Yes
Professional grooming	If needed, for special cases	May offer to transport
Transportation (to foster, medical appointments, adoption events, etc.)	May arrange for transportation	May volunteer to transport
Public adoption events	May hold public adoption events	May volunteer at event or only drop off/pick up foster dog
Medical care (basic)	Provides in-home medications (dewormer, flea meds, topical meds)	Administers in-home medications
Medical care (extensive)	Arranges for and pays for care. Communicates directly with veterinarian	Follows veterinarian instructions at home
Nutrition	Yes	May volunteer to provide food and treats
Supplies	Yes	May volunteer to provide supplies

If you are a first time foster, my recommendation is, again, that you foster an easy dog. By this, I mean a dog that has relatively low needs, as far as time, medication, and supplies are concerned. Start off with a dog who only needs basic medical care (spay/neuter, vaccinations, and microchip), doesn't have serious behavioral training needs, doesn't require an hour of exercise daily, and who is likely to be adopted within a month or two. Although you likely can take on more, consider this a learning experience. A good rescue will want you to have a positive experience and then foster another dog for you in the future.

Case Study #2 (continued) - *Rachel, Rocky, and "the ladies" are getting along swimmingly. Rachel has let the rescue coordinator know that she is fine with purchasing Rocky's special dog food. The rescue organization was very responsive when Rocky developed a limp and needed to be seen by a veterinarian. After three months, Rocky's coat has become shiny and bright - he even smells good since she gave him a good bath. For the most part, Rocky has been an easy houseguest. There have been a couple of applications for his adoption, but neither was a great match. Rachel is prepared for Rocky's placement to take another three or six months, or even more.*

Rachel now gets messages through the rescue organization's mailing list. One message highlights a dog in need of a foster or an adopter- a senior yorkie who was relinquished to the shelter because of a severe heart murmur. The dog, Mimi, is very sick and needs a quiet place to live out the rest of her life. Rachel's heart broke for Mimi but she is also unsure about fostering a dog that could die in her care. She reaches out to the rescue coordinator regarding hospice care for Mimi. They agree that Rachel's home is the calm and quiet place that Mimi needs. On the call, Rachel communicates that she will need ongoing support and help with veterinary care, but that she is confident in giving Mimi her oral medications. Soon afterwards, Mimi arrives at Rachel's house to receive the generous

WHAT ARE YOU WILLING TO GIVE?

gift of selfless care.

8

Selecting a Rescue

Let's talk about selecting a rescue. There are three ways in which you can come across a dog rescue. First, you can volunteer at a municipal shelter which has a foster program. Second, you can find a rescue from social media, such as NextDoor, Facebook, or Instagram. Third, you can identify rescues through pet adoption websites.

You can find out if your local brick-and-mortar animal shelter has a foster program by looking at their website. Information would be found as part of the volunteer program information page. Animal shelters will offer volunteer training and may ask for a minimum commitment (in hours or months). They may require on-site volunteer hours prior to allowing a volunteer to qualify for the at-home foster program. Although the local humane society or city animal services department will likely require more paperwork and training, there are distinct benefits. For example, you will be introduced to other ways to donate time, you will meet other volunteers like yourself, and you will have the support of full-time shelter staff.

On the other hand, you may already have a rescue in mind. If you are networked through Next Door, Facebook, or Instagram, you may occasionally see someone asking for someone to foster a dog. If you see a dog or an organization on social media, and you would like to help foster, you can reach out directly to the poster in an instant message. Be cautious to make sure that the dog is associated with a 501c3 nonprofit rescue. Sometimes people find lost dogs, cannot keep their dog, or are trying to help a shelter dog and will ask people to help. Unfortunately, without the safety net of a registered rescue group, you will be responsible for all of the medical care, training, networking, and the adoption process. Many people do this, and it is called independent rescue, but I do not recommend it for an inexperienced foster.

The best way to find a breed-specific rescue is through an internet search. The American Kennel Club lists some purebred rescue groups, and there are many more local affiliates in each state. For example you might be interested in helping Siberian huskies and you live in Arizona. A search for "Arizona husky rescue" brings up www.azhuskyrescue.com. The website identifies that the group is registered as a 501c3 nonprofit, has a "contact us" button, outlines their requirements for fosters, and has a foster application.

Another way to find a breed-specific or nonspecific rescue is through pet adoption websites. These are websites where shelters and rescue groups list their dogs available for adoption. Each group will have their own account where they can list the dog's location, age, breed, sex, and personality traits, along with some photos and a brief bio. It's a bit like online dating for dogs, because people can search locally or nation-wide for their perfect pet.

The two most well known pet adoption websites are Petfinder and Adopt a Pet. Both websites have an option for searching for a rescue by location. From there, you can click on the names of groups to see more information, including which animals are currently with that rescue and how many animals each rescue currently has in their care, and the group's contact information. As another option, you can find a group by looking at the dogs listed on the website. For example, I can search for dogs within 25 miles of my zip code that are large (61-100 lbs). That will bring up a list of dogs in my area. I see that there are several large dogs available through a group called "Amazing Dogs". I can click on their website link to see more about their mission, their available dogs, and find more information on fostering. Their website specifies some of the expectations for their fosters, such as that dogs typically need 4-8 weeks in foster and that fosters are expected to bring dogs to adoption events. Finally, there is a foster application available on the website.

I recommend, for a new foster, that you start off by asking around for recommendations in your immediate area. Do you know someone who has adopted a rescue dog? Ask them about their experience interacting with the group. If your friend had a positive interaction then you most likely will, too. If your friend felt lost in the adoption process, you might feel lost in the fostering process. Look at groups that are in a convenient location, so that transportation to and from veterinary clinics and adoption events will not be an issue. If they have a website, read through the available information to see if there are indications of expectations. Finally, start with just one group. Volunteering for more than one rescue can cause logistical issues. You can always change groups at a later time.

Case Study #3 - Lawrence. As a father of two teenage boys, Lawrence doesn't have a lot of time on his hands. But both boys have approached Lawrence about fostering for a rescue as a family. Their current dog, Lacey, is a six year old golden retriever mix who loves snowy winters and summers swimming in the lake. Lacey is a "daddy's girl" and Lawrence has a soft spot for golden retrievers in general. One day the boys presented Lawrence with a little presentation about dog rescue and the need for more foster families. Lawrence is so touched by his sons' empathy that he agrees to try out fostering, if they can find a local golden retriever rescue. They go online together, searching for "Tulsa Golden Retriever Rescue". Within minutes they come across the website for Sooner Golden Retriever Rescue. All three are impressed with the detailed information on the website, with the number of dogs that have been rescued by the organization, and by the many ways to volunteer. Lawrence fills out the foster application on the website and waits to hear back from Sooner. Before going to bed, he gives Lacey a couple of extra treats, grateful that she has inspired his love for all goldens.

HOW TO FOSTER A RESCUE DOG

9

Reaching Out

Once you have chosen a group for whom you would like to volunteer, the next step is reaching out. Some groups will have an email or phone contact online, while others will have foster applications available on their website. The application form can be quite extensive, asking questions about your household, your other pets, and your training experience. The purpose of these questions are to make sure that the foster dog will be safe and will be a good fit for your lifestyle.

In contacting a rescue via email, you will want to help demonstrate that you have a safe and stable home where a dog will receive the care that he needs. Here is an example of an email you might send to a rescue organization in reaching out regarding fostering. Feel free to use some of the wording if you need help getting started on your own message.

Dear ___(rescue organization)_____,
 I am interested in fostering a dog for your rescue. I have

always valued animal rescue and have hoped to help save a dog in need. I live in _____ with my husband and fifteen year old daughter. We rent our home and have permission from the landlord to have two dogs. Our townhouse is two stories and a small enclosed patio. My husband works 6-3, our daughter is in school from 8-4, and I work from home Monday through Friday 9-6. Our family is all on the same page about fostering a dog.

We have one other pet, an 8 year old beagle mix named Pugsley. He is neutered, up to date on shots, and social with other dogs. We took him to some training classes when he was young and we have had him for seven years. Puggsley has an area on the patio where he potties but also enjoys going for walks. We plan to have the foster dog follow his schedule for potty time and other routines. The house and the patio are both very secure.

Sometimes our dog can be fearful of large dogs, so we would prefer to foster a small or medium sized dog, up to 30 pounds. Since this is our first venture into fostering, we would prefer a male or female dog who is friendly, playful, over one year of age. We have a crate from when our dog was younger, so we can crate train the foster. We can provide the foster with dry food and toys, unless there is specific food that the rescue requires. We may need help with transporting the dog for veterinary appointments due to work schedules. We will also need help with dog sitting the foster dog if he or she is still with us past the first week of June, since we have a week-long vacation planned for after school is out.

We look forward to hearing back from you regarding volunteering to foster for your rescue organization. Hopefully, we will learn a lot in the process and help a dog in need. Thank you for all that you do for the dogs!

Take care,

___(potential foster)___

This may seem like a lot to write, and it may seem like the potential foster is being a bit picky, but it would greatly help the foster coordinator in the organization to match up the right dog with this new volunteer. By giving the rescue coordinator more information, you're letting them know that you have thought hard about volunteering and you are ready to commit. You've thought about the dog's safety, home environment, and your ability to care for him. You have also stated your boundaries, requirements, and what you are willing to give. Online foster applications are often even more detailed, asking for specific information on the height of your fence and your experience with dog training. Start off with good communication towards the rescue and expect good communication from the rescue.

If you live within a reasonable distance from the rescue's main headquarters and if they are actively looking for fosters, then it is highly likely that you will hear back from the rescue. The onboarding process varies from one rescue to the next. You may be asked to fill out their foster application if you haven't already. Someone from the organization will likely call you and have a phone conversation to get to know you and they may want to visit your home to verify that the space is safe and the yard is secure. On the other hand, your first contact with the rescue may be from a coordinator who asks you if and when you can take a particular dog who is in need of a foster home.

However the rescue group reaches out, this is the right time to talk with them about the kind of dog you would like to foster, what you are willing to give, and what support you will need. Ask if they have any sort of training documents for new fosters. Ask if they will transport and provide food or if you are required to do this. Ask if the person calling you is your main point of contact and get their number. Ask if there is another foster in the group who can mentor you. This is the best way to clarify expectations and avoid isolation. If you are comfortable with the way that they are communicating with you and are confident that this is the right rescue for you, then you should proceed with making arrangements for your new foster dog. If not, then it's ok to tell the volunteer that you are also considering other rescue groups and you can't commit at this time. Then, reach out to your second or third choice rescue group.

I personally recommend that you treat the initial interaction with a rescue group as a mutual interview. If you put your best foot forward in the application process but don't hear back for a week or two, then that could be a sign that the group is understaffed and slow to respond to potential adopters as well. If the first call from the rescue is a desperate plea to take in a particular dog, regardless of your experience level or preferences, then that could indicate a lack of appreciation for your boundaries. If their expectation is that you pay for all supplies and do all of the transport, but you've asked for assistance, then you could be financially stressed in volunteering for this particular group. Make a connection with the volunteer coordinator and go with your gut when it comes to making a commitment. Whichever group you choose to volunteer for needs your help to save more dogs. Just be sure that you understand their process and you can commit to their program.

Case Study #3 (Continued). A few days after reaching out to Sooner Retriever Rescue, a volunteer coordinator, Sharon, calls Lawrence to follow up. He and Sharon have a good talk, connecting about kids and dogs. Sharon asks him some specific questions regarding who will take care of the dog – Lawrence or the kids. Knowing he already does most of Lacey's care, and understanding that the kids are too young to be volunteer fosters, Lawrence reassures Sharon that he will be responsible. Sharon appreciates Lawrence's prior golden retriever experience and she asks what age range, energy level, and sex he would be open to fostering. Golden retriever puppies can be a handful, he says, so he would prefer a dog out of the puppy stage (male or female). This is a good opportunity for Lawrence to ask questions as well. He asks about his responsibilities (financial, time commitment, and medical), about the rescue's adoption procedures, and about supplies for the foster.

By the end of the conversation, both Lawrence and Sharon have had the opportunity to have all their questions answered. It might be a few weeks before the right foster dog is ready for Lawrence, but he is pre-approved as a volunteer foster. In the meantime, Sharon will be sending him additional information, including an additional form. To finalize the approval, Sharon and Lawrence arrange for a time when she can do a home check, to verify a safe home environment and to connect in person. Although a bit overwhelmed, Lawrence is excited to share the news with his boys when they come home.

REACHING OUT

10

Preparing to Bring Home Your Foster

Now that you've found a rescue group you like, and you've agreed to be a part of their team, it's time to get ready to bring home the dog. The group may have a training or orientation guideline, or may even have in-person training. In my experience, the orientation is typically the phone call, signing a foster agreement, and maybe a home check to make sure the dog will be safe. In any case, you should have a point of contact for asking questions regarding the organization's expectations, policies, and procedures. Now that the rescue has you on board as a volunteer, and they know your qualifications, they will be able to say "yes" to a dog in need. It's time to get prepared!

Is your home ready for this change? You'll probably need to dog-proof a few things. Double check that the home is secure. Here is a list of some things to check as part of preparing your home.

- Does the front door securely latch?

- Are any screens easily pushed out when a window is open?
- Are there any loose boards in the fence?
- Do you see any holes under the fence where the dog could squeeze out?
- Are there planters, pots, or tables near the fence which could help the dog jump over it?
- Do kitchen cupboards close all the way and stay shut?
- Are childrens' toys put away?
- Are shoes put away into closets?
- Are any small pets (birds, hamsters, lizards) in a safe place where a dog can't reach them?
- Are there any tempting and valuable chew-able items in low places?
- Are there any of your plants toxic to dogs?
- Are there any easily accessible foods or other items which are toxic to dogs?
- Is the cat litter box difficult for the dog to access?
- Are there any loose boards in the fence?
- Do you see any holes under the fence where the dog could squeeze out?
- Are there planters, pots, or tables near the fence which could help the dog jump over it?
- Is there a lock on the gate?
- Is the pool secured?
- Are there objects that are sharp/dangerous where the dog might harm himself?
- Is there a location outside the apartment/condo where the dog can potty?

You'll notice that a lot of the dog-proofing checks are focused around keeping the dog from escaping. You'll need to see your home through the lens of an animal who tries to get back to where he used to be. Rescue dogs are more likely than other pets to try to escape. They are coming into your home as a stranger, and they might try to get back to their last owner (the one who abandoned them at the shelter, dumped them in a field, or relinquished them to the rescue). They just do not understand that their person isn't waiting for them to come home. They also may be familiar with wandering free as a stray. A dog who has been living somewhat self-sustainably on the streets could be a bit reluctant to change his wandering ways. For many reasons, your new foster may be an escape artist, tunnel digger, or door dasher and it is your new job to outsmart him.

If your children are used to going out the front door without making sure it is closed behind them, have a talk with them. Make sure they understand the importance of blocking the dog from following them as they leave and closing the door securely. If you have a gardener or utility person who accesses your yard on occasion, you'll need to close the dog inside during those hours. I've had a couple of dogs run down the street after an unsuspecting gardener came through the gate at an earlier than usual time. It's best practice is to keep a lock on your gate and only take off the lock when the dog is inside the house. If you use a dog door, make sure you have the insert to block the door when necessary.

Other dog-proofing checks are focused around keeping the dog from chewing on items that are either dangerous to him or precious to you. I had one dog open the kitchen cupboard and help herself to whatever she wanted. I came home to find her with a five pound bag of flour. It looked like a scene from Scarface. I've had to call the ASPCA Animal Poison Control helpline [(888)426-4435] after chocolates were stolen from a Christmas Stocking. I've had flip-flops, socks, bras, and cash destroyed. Just recently, my husband's expensive sunglasses were chewed up by our foster puppy. It was his responsibility not to leave them on the coffee table where the puppy could get them, but it was still an upsetting loss (one which cost me a pretty penny to replace). If your foster dog chews up something it shouldn't have, you really can't blame the dog. Your foster dog is clueless as to what is okay to chew and what is not. You are much smarter. You are capable of providing things that are on the "ok" list, redirecting inappropriate chewing, and putting tennis shoes in the closet. As an aside, the rescue will not reimburse you for destroyed property, including sunglasses.

On the topic of providing things that are okay to chew, you'll also need some supplies in preparation for bringing home your foster dog. Starting with escape preparation, I recommend that you get a pet gate. This can also be a baby gate or some other way to limit the dog's access to areas of the house. For me, I use a dog gate between the kitchen and the living room. I use it to sequester the dogs behind the gate when there is a lot of activity at the front door (such as pizza delivery or bringing in the groceries). If you have a two-story house, you might use a gate to keep the dog on one floor of the house. Do you have a cat? Having a way to separate the cat (and her litter box!) from the foster dog is important for both species. Having ways to control the space that the dog is allowed to explore is quite important for acclimating the dog to your home, which we'll get to later.

Second, I highly recommend getting a wire dog crate. The rescue should supply this. If not, it's worth the $100 investment.

Crate training will give the dog routine, prevent potty accidents, reduce unwanted chewing, and give the dog a safe space of his own. Ask the rescue coordinator for guidance on the appropriate size of crate for your first foster.

Third, you'll need some generalized dog items. Here is a basic list so that you're prepared.

- Dog collar and tag: Your foster dog will need a collar with an identification tag in case he escapes your home
- Harness or martingale collar: Many people prefer a harness for walks. It is easier on the dog's neck if he is a puller and also avoids the risk of the dog slipping out of the collar. A martingale collar will also prevent the dog from wiggling out of the collar if he is stressed or scared.
- Leash: A four or six foot nylon or leather leash, not a retractable one.
- Poop bags: Always clean up after your dog. Earth Rated makes compostable poop bags.
- Dog bed: A dog bed is important for the dog's comfort. I usually go to Costco or Home Goods for the best deals.
- Food and water bowls: Choose durable and easy to clean bowls that are difficult to tip over and easy to fill. Discount stores like Marshalls and HomeGoods or the local Goodwill often have plenty of dog bowls available.
- High quality dog food: Talk with the rescue about the food that they recommend, if they will supply the food, and about how much your foster should be fed daily
- Treats: Useful for rewarding good behavior and for training
- Chew toys: Useful for encouraging chewing on appropriate things. I recommend Kong Classic toys, since they are

difficult to destroy and easy to fill with soft treats
- Grooming supplies: Depending on the dog, you may need a brush, nail clippers, and shampoo. Earth Bath makes biodegradable shampoos. Their fragrance free hypoallergenic shampoo is a good choice for most dogs.
- Training supplies: Depending on the dog you get, you might need potty pads, a clicker, a treat pouch, or other supplies.
- Dewormer and flea and tick treatment: Ask the rescue if the dog will already be treated for worms and fleas before you get him. If the answer is no, ask that they provide you with these medications before you get him, at the time that you receive him, or, at the very least, on the day that you get him.

The rescue might provide you with a starter kit containing a leash, food, some toys, etc., or they may ask what you need and only supply those items. If you already have a dog of your own, you probably already have a dog water bowl, treats, and beds. Communicate clearly what you have and what you need. By all means, do not go on a shopping spree and send the bill to the rescue! That receipt will only be good for tax purposes.

PREPARING TO BRING HOME YOUR FOSTER

11

Bringing Home Your Foster

What do you do when the time has come? Either you're on your way to pick up your foster dog or someone is bringing the dog to you. On the day of arrival, you'll want the home to be a calm environment. If you have a cat, the cat should be safely sequestered away in a bedroom with everything she needs to thrive while ignoring the dog. If you have one or more dogs of your own, you'll want the dog(s) to be away from the front door, in a back room. It's best if you don't have house guests or a birthday party going on.

You'll meet the person who has your foster dog. This could be a transporter, someone in your community, a shelter worker, or a coordinator from the rescue. Instead of just transferring the dog, use this as your opportunity to learn anything you can about the dog. Ask the person who now has the dog what they know about his background, if he rides in the car well, if he was barking on the way, etc. This person may just know that the dog smells and threw up in the back seat on his ride over to your house. They may also know how the dog was relinquished, if he has siblings in the rescue, if there are signs of illness, if he has been treated for worms/fleas and if he needs an identification tag. The background of your new house guest is a mystery. Look for clues along the way which might help you.

Case Study #4 - Earl - Today is the day! After meeting up with the local mixed breed rescue, he is ready to receive a male, medium sized corgi mix. Knowing that corgis can be quite smart, Steve has prepared his condo for anything. The kitchen trash can was replaced with one that has a lid, to prevent dumpster diving. He installed a baby gate between the living room and the hallway. And, best yet, he took this as an opportunity to fully clean the bedroom - including under the bed. His cat, Mochi, is all set up in the office with her litter box, food, and scratching post. Mochi will get some good 1:1 time when Earl calls in for Zoom meetings.

There's a ring at the door. The transporter is there with a friendly, rather portly, corgi mix. In their conversation, Earl learns that the dog came from a rural shelter and has a number, no name. He had been listed for euthanasia, but the shelter staff loved his personality so much that they used their network to reach out to rescues in the area. Because Earl decided to foster, there was availability for the corgi rescue group to take in the dog. He rode well in the car and was full of kisses. That's all Earl learned about his new guest before he confidently waddled in the door and started sniffing around. Well, Earl thought to himself, I guess we're roommates now!

When the foster dog is at my house, I like to start by taking him around to the back yard and letting him smell and go potty. If you do not have a yard, then take the dog to the area where he will be going potty so that he can take in all of the scents and relieve himself. It may have been a long car ride for the pup. By letting the dog sniff around the yard, you're giving him a chance to know if other dogs are present. Male dogs, in particular, seem to enjoy the opportunity to sniff the yard and lift their leg wherever our dog Wally has peed. One advantage of letting a dog potty outside before coming inside is that he is less likely to have an accident (or an "on purpose") when he comes inside the house.

Next, if he'll let me, I'll spend some time petting him and giving him treats. Now, if he hasn't been dewormed already (check with the rescue!) I'll slip a dewormer pill in with one of the treats. If he has no fleas but needs topical flea treatment, I'll slyly put that on him while I'm petting him. If I notice fleas on his belly while giving it a rub, I'll know that he needs a bath right away. Petting the dog helps him to bond with you and also gives you the opportunity to check his coat for fleas, ticks, and matted fur. You can look for fleas on his skin, scabs due to fleas, or "flea dirt" around the ears and at the base of the tail. You can also feel for lumps, bumps, scars, scabs, and ticks. If you find something concerning, let the rescue coordinator know right away. Just be aware - you may need to treat the dog for fleas, ticks, or worms before introducing him to your dog, cat, or kids.

What you do next will depend on whether you have a dog of your own. First, let's cover what happens if you do have a dog. Some rescues will require that you keep the foster dog sequestered from your dog until the dog is known to be healthy and social. This keeps your dog safe from illness and harm. Follow the rescue coordinator's advice on when/if the foster can be introduced to your dog. The same goes for cats. There is a lot of information available on cat-dog introductions, but for the first two weeks of having your foster you shouldn't consider introducing them. Cats can get very upset and display negative behaviors if a new animal is in their territory. Give the cat a dog-free zone at least until she shows interest in meeting the dog. Dog-cat and dog-dog introductions could be a book all to itself!

Case study #4 - Continued. It didn't take long for Earl's new buddy, now named Hank, to make himself at home. They spent the first night getting to know each other. According to the shelter paperwork, Hank had been treated for fleas, ticks, and kennel cough. He was released without being neutered, so the corgi rescue needed to get that done asap. Hank shed like the dickens. As Earl brushed Hank with his cat, Mochi's, pin brush (to do: get dog brush!) a ball of fur the size of a hamster came off of the dog. But Hank loved being brushed. He gladly rolled onto his back for Earl to brush his belly. Earl looked at Hank's skin, ears, and teeth without a problem. Besides being a fat little barrel of a dog, and shedding another whole handful of undercoat, Hank seemed to be in good condition.

Hank was definitely a smart dog. He went potty out on the back patio and happily lounged in his crate the first night. The next morning he knew to follow Earl to the back door to go to the patio. Good dog! Earl decided to just let Hank roam freely while he got ready for work. Suddenly he heard some high pitched barks from down the hallway. "Mochi! Oh no, is Hank harassing Mochi!?" He thought to himself as he looked to make sure the office was still closed. Indeed it was, and there was Hank, lying on his side, peeking under the doorway. He had obviously noticed the cat, and, from the looks of it, the cat had noticed him, too. Mochi was playfully reaching under the door to bop Hank on the nose and paws. "To do – Google cat-dog introductions" Hank thought. Who knew Mochi would show interest in interacting with the foster dog?

When it is time to introduce the foster dog to the resident dog, it is best to do introductions on a neutral territory with lots of praise and positive reinforcement. As long as your dog is not leash aggressive towards other dogs, you can try having two people walk them at the same time. Start off with the dogs very far apart – several houses away from each other or on opposite sides of the street. As you walk, gradually decrease the distance between the dogs. Look for signs of aggression, such growling, raised fur on the back, snapping, and certain barks (like the kind you'd hear if the mailman was at the door). Also look for signs of either dog being afraid or overwhelmed, such as body tension, refusing to move forward, cowering, trying to get further from the other dog, whining, and barking (the high pitched kind that says "stay back, give me space!"). If there are signs of aggression, fear, or feeling overwhelmed, then increase the distance between the dogs. Only after the two dogs can happily walk together in a pack should you consider letting them off leash in your yard or home.

Now, let's consider the case where there is no other dog and/or there are other people in the household. Introducing the dog to other people should be done in a calm way. You all may want to shower the dog with kisses and pets. Some dogs are ready for that on day one. But most foster dogs are a bit anxious when they go to their foster family's home. They are often undersocialized and unsure about these new people. Consider what it would be like to be plopped into a foreign country where you don't know the language and everyone wants to touch you. This dog doesn't know if you are a threat or a friend. The two things that help to reassure the dog are time and consistency.

When your family meets the dog, tell them just to hang out and ignore it. For example, have a conversation, all sitting together in the living room, with the dog present. Pretend the dog isn't there. Let the dog sniff you without the threat that you'll touch him or stare at him. What really helps is if the people have several small treats. Don't require the dog to take them from your hands, just drop them near you occasionally. Gradually a shy dog will associate tasty treats with your presence and warm up to you.

Now, I know that every dog is different. Your first foster dog might be the exact opposite - a party in a small package who immediately greets your dog, jumps in your partner's lap, gets belly rubs from the kids, and runs off playing with your favorite toy. In this case, congratulations. You asked for an easy dog and you got one. Sailing though introductions feels incredibly encouraging for any foster parent.

There is a saying that goes like this: It takes 3 days to decompress, 3 weeks to learn a new routine, and 3 months to start to feel at home. The first three days in your home, your foster may still feel quite overwhelmed, unsure where the next meal will come from, compelled to hide or escape, depressed, and just not comfortable enough to be himself/herself. Go slow and give him time. I've had dogs cry at the front window and then go curl up in a ball and refuse to eat. I had a chihuahua crawl inside the mechanism of the recliner like a cat. I've had dogs who had apparently never lived inside because they were too afraid to come in the back door. All of these dogs were resilient enough to warm up to me within a few days' time.

<u>Case Study #5 -Yan and Andrew.</u> *Yan and her husband Andrew have decided to foster for their local county shelter. They have already attended the Saturday afternoon training at the shelter, filled out paperwork, and purchased the list of needed supplies. Today, they are on their way to the shelter to pick up Bubba, a goofy rottweiler mix who was neutered this morning. Before leaving the house, they put their lab, Willow, in the bedroom, cleaned up the house, closed interior doors, put up a baby gate at the stairway, and set up his dog crate. They have a dog crate in the back of the SUV – the one they use for Willlow when they take her camping. When they arrive at the shelter, they are greeted by a lethargic boy who is in need of a bath and a few extra meals.*

As Yan fills out the paperwork, Andrew talks with the shelter technician about Bubba. How has he been with other dogs? Does he eat well? Any signs of kennel cough? Is he friendly with visitors? He tells the tech that this is his first foster dog and they reassure him that the foster coordinator set them up with a gentle giant. Yan smiles, because that's just her type of dog. On the way home, Bubba whines a little, probably because of the effects of the anesthesia. They bring him around the back yard where he sniffs around and pees a river. Bubba plops himself down in the middle of the lawn, feeling the grass tickle his cheeks as he rubs his head back and forth. Yan and Andrew sit with him a while, petting his greasy fur and feeling his calloused paws. Bubba's ears are a bit dirty but his neuter incision looks ok. Yan says to Andrew, "Bubba's going to be a very good pet for someone. Until then, we'll give him all the time and love he needs to be happy and healthy." Andrew nods understandingly, happy they made the decision to foster for the local shelter.

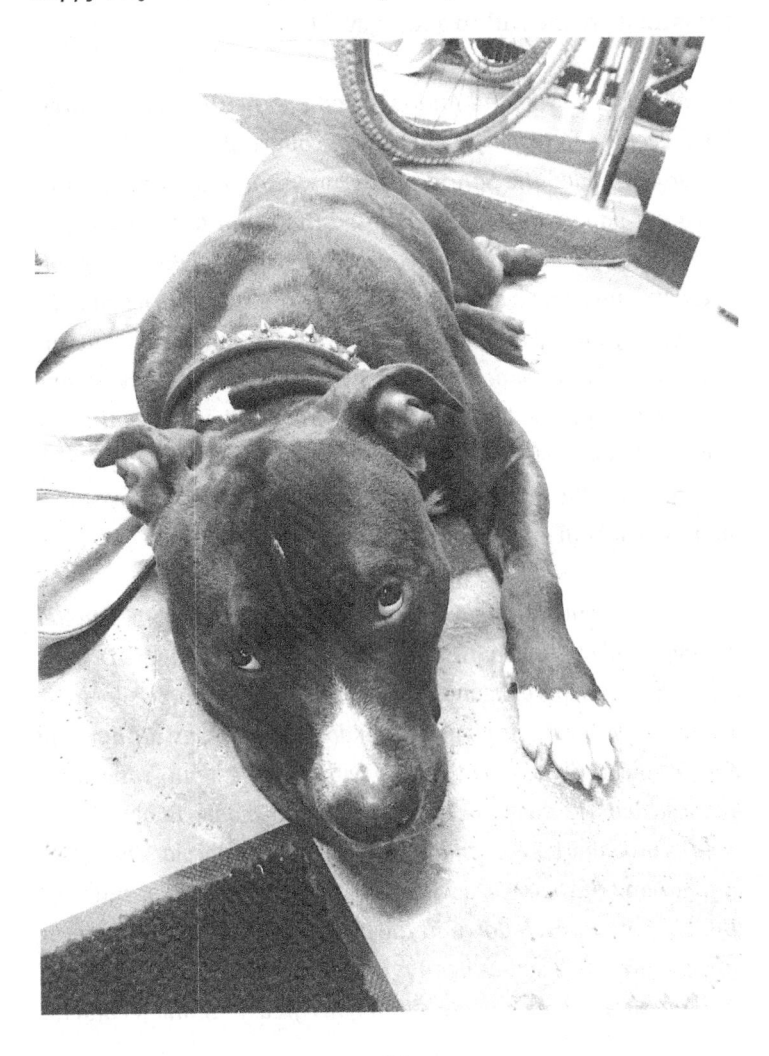

12

Caring for Your Foster Dog

While the foster dog is in your care, you are fully responsible for their well-being. The rescue owns the dog, but the foster is responsible for the dog's safety, daily routine, training, socialization, and monitoring. I like to treat the foster dog as one of my pack, although I know that their stay is only temporary.

Safety

You should have already dog-proofed your home prior the foster's arrival, and every day you will want to keep an eye out for the dog's safety. It is such a horrible feeling as a foster when your dog has escaped your home and you are frantically searching the neighborhood for it. I've been there and, luckily the dog had a tag with the group's phone number on it. A neighbor called the rescue and I sheepishly went over to pick him up. For the dog's safety, keep a watchful eye at the front door, or, better yet, keep the foster behind a baby gate when there is activity at the front door.

What's worse is the horror of seeing your foster get into a fight with a resident dog or cat and needing medical attention. Taking introductions slowly and separating dogs when you're not home can help mitigate this risk. Likewise, interactions between the foster and children should be monitored. Children should be taught to respect the dog's personal space, to be gentle, to watch for warning signs that the dog is nervous, and to ask permission prior to interacting with a new dog. Avoiding a negative interaction is much easier than dealing with a dog bite. Dogs do better with baby steps than with being thrown off the deep end. Set them up for success by being safe and going slowly.

Routine

The longer that you have your foster, the more you can predict how they will react to different situations and the more they will predict your routine. Dogs are creatures of habit and like to know what is predictably coming in the future. They look for patterns in your day to see what will be coming next for them. I've had dogs start begging for dinner around dusk because they know they get fed at night time. I've also had a dog who would start whining in her crate earlier and earlier in the morning because I would take her out to potty first thing and she liked to try to play during those potty breaks. It is up to the foster to set the daily routine for the dog.

In our case, we have the advantage of having two very friendly dogs, our fosters have not been dog-dog aggressive, and we did introductions early. Having another dog friend seems to help the foster dog to decompress and learn the routines. We all go out to the yard to potty first thing in the morning, last thing at night, and at least once mid-day. The dogs eat at the same time, twice a day, in designated locations. When it comes to toys and beds and furniture, it's a bit of "monkey see monkey do". My dogs are allowed on the furniture under certain conditions and the foster will join them. If you do not have a resident dog, try to build a new routine with your foster dog: potty time, eating time, rest and snuggle time, etc. The more the foster dog can predict what is coming next, the less anxious he will feel. That takes time.

Boundaries

Along with routine, boundaries also help to assure a smooth transition. Don't give your foster dog run of the house and yard at first. Close doors to some rooms until the dog has gotten used to the main rooms. Keep closet doors closed. Watch him when he's outside and bring him in when you go inside. Except for introductions with your dog, don't take the foster on walks for the first week or two. Don't take rides in the car unless it's to go to the vet. Certainly don't go to the dog park or the pet food store or your best friend's house. Keep their world small. Your foster needs to get used to the routine in this small world before adding on anything new. He needs to trust you and know that he is safe here before he faces challenges out in the world.

Socialization

Foster dogs come from various situations which are likely quite different from what they are experiencing now. Your foster may have no experience with living in a house, living in a neighborhood, seeing cars race by, hearing loud noises, greeting strangers, seeing other dogs, or taking rides in the car. All of the things we take for granted might be completely new to this dog. I once had a dog get spooked by a garden gnome. I've had fosters who did not understand that dogs could come inside.

One foster would go flat on his belly out of fright every time a loud truck went by. By socializing your foster dog in basic ways.

Socialization entails introducing the dog to new experiences and creating positive association with those new experiences. Praise your foster and give them treats for trying new things. If you see them timidly go up the front steps, lavish them with praise for giving it a go. If they are afraid of the vacuum, keep treats in your pocket and toss them towards the dog as you clean. When the dog seems curious about the sounds coming out of the dishwasher or the popcorn maker or the blender, give lots of treats and praise. I had a dog so afraid of the coffee grinder than he would hide under the bed. By bringing out the best treats when the grinder came on, I eventually had all the dogs running to the kitchen whenever I made coffee. Consistent positive associations can greatly improve any dog's confidence.

Once your foster has mastered the house, try some socialization exercises outside the house. Go for rides in the car, praising the dog for getting into the car. Take walks around the neighborhood, observing the dog's behavior and encouraging bravery when there is a challenging situation. I once had a foster dog get so spooked by a statue of a woman in front of a garden center.. I encouraged him to check her out. He very slowly approached, almost crawling up to her. Once he realized it wasn't a real person, he wagged his tail and proudly walked off while taking treats and high praise. The next time we encountered the same statue he did not react at all. Helping the foster become more confident in the world around him will make him much more adoptable and give him a head start in that new life. Just be aware - dogs should not be forced to encounter new things.

Avoid creating that negative association.

Some fosters will get excited and socialize the dog towards other peoples' dogs, strangers, and various new environments. I'd like to caution you regarding taking too many chances with your foster dog. Your primary responsibility is to keep the dog safe, and places like dog parks, off-leash dog beaches, crowded events, and wilderness hikes can be very risky. Focus on neighborhood dog walks in areas where you can keep the dog safely distanced from other dogs, skateboards, squirrels, children, rattlesnakes, and natural hazards. Check in with the rescue group prior to taking your foster to a dog park.

Case Study #5 (Continued) - It's been about a week since Yan and Andrew brought home Bubba. They have carefully introduced him to Willow and the biggest hazard so far has been the thunder of their paws as they chase each other up and down the hall. Keeping Bubba calm after his neuter surgery has been difficult since he does love to play with Willow, so they keep him crated when they are not home. Overall, the transition has gone well. Bubba follows Willow outside to go potty, eats his meals with glee, and even tolerated a wipe-down with some wet towels. He has tried to take over Andrew's recliner but is easily redirected to the dog bed. Socialization in the home has gone very well.

Training

Nobody expects a fully trained dog when they adopt one from a rescue. But some training will be necessary in order to integrate the dog into your home and into their adoptive home as well. We already discussed positive association with socialization. I also suggest working on crate training, potty training, eating at mealtime, the sit command, and walking nicely on leash.

Crate Training

Boundaries and routine can also be reinforced with crate training. Crate training is beyond the scope of this book, but here are the basic steps for crate training.

Choose a crate that is the right size for your foster dog, with enough room for them to stand up, turn around, and lie down comfortably. Place the crate in a common area and leave the door open. There should be soft bedding material, such as a dog blanket, in the bottom of the crate. I also like to put a towel or blanket over the top of the crate, making a more den-like environment. Make a positive association with the crate. Put some toys and treats in the crate, leaving the door open, so that the dog can voluntarily explore the crate. At meal time, feed the dog inside the crate. Gradually increase crate time. For a foster dog, you'll need him to sleep in the crate at night. You will also want to use the crate to confine the dog when you go out for a few hours, to avoid potty mishaps and chewing incidents. Always praise the dog for going in the crate and reward with a treat.

Ignore whining or barking. It may be difficult, but if the dog whines or barks, do not respond since that will reinforce the behavior. The dog should eventually self-soothe and relax. At night, I like to put the crate in the bedroom if I have a particularly anxious dog, in case there is whining or barking. Then I can reach my hand down and help soothe the dog until he gets acclimated to the crate. Be patient and consistent. Crate training takes time and patience. The goal is to have a dog who understands the routine and sees the crate as his little den.

The crate should never be used as punishment. It is a tool for the dog's safety, security, happiness, training, routine, and, ultimately, transition. This will help with his next transition, to the adopter's home, when they have a crate for him, too. Dogs in my house tend to make a positive association with the crate. The interior is soft and comfy, with a blanket over the top of it so it feels more secure like a den. Dogs are never forced to be closed in there for long periods of time during the day, but they have access to the crate and can go there whenever they want. Often I'll find one of our own dogs snoozing in the foster dog's crate. I once put a foster dog in the crate at night not knowing that our small dog was already in there and they slept together there all night. Make positive associations with the crate and encourage the adopters to have one so that the dog will have a consistent routine after the transition.

If you have concerns and need more guidance, please consult resources from professional trainers. I've also added additional information resources at the end of this book.

Potty Training

One of the most frequent questions I get from potential adopters is "Is he potty trained?" My answer is always candid. I'll let them know how the dog has been doing at our house (mostly consistent, with encouragement, with a couple of accidents) and emphasize that potty training will need to be reinforced in their home. Even adult dogs, who have previously understood potty training, occasionally have accidents in new environments.

With potty training, establish a routine. Take the dog out at regular intervals, such as first thing in the morning, after meals, and before bedtime. Puppies need to go out even more frequently. Take the puppy's age, in months, and double the number. That's about how many hours the puppy can hold it. A four month old puppy might be able to make it through the night without going out, but might not. On the other side of the spectrum, senior dogs sometimes need more frequent potty trips. Be ready to adjust the potty schedule depending on the dog's needs.

Even if the dog has open access to the yard, it is important to go out with them and make a positive association with going potty outside. Use a consistent command, such as "go potty" or "do your business" and use it every time you take the dog outside. When they go potty, reward the behavior with praise and treats or playtime. This will help them associate going potty outside with positive experiences. As mentioned earlier, limit their access in the house to just a few rooms until you are confident that they will not go potty inside. While training, watch for signs that the dog needs to go potty, such as sniffing or whining. If you notice signs, take them outside. Finally, be patient. Potty training a puppy or an adult dog can take some time. Keep in mind that accidents will happen and have some good quality enzymatic cleaner for cleaning up messes. Just remember that each dog is different. Some may immediately go to the back door and bark when they need to go out. Others will go off to a place where you can't see them, like the laundry room, and have an accident. If you're feeling frustrated or having issues succeeding, reach out to the rescue for additional support.

Eating at Mealtime

Many people do what is called "free feeding" for their dog. This is when a bowl of food is left out and the dog eats as much as they would like to at any time of day. This method can make it difficult to know how much the dog is eating, particularly if there are multiple dogs in the house. Knowing how much the dog is eating is also important if the dog needs to gain or lose weight. I prefer to use a measuring cup for each dog's food and feed them twice a day. This gives me the ability to adjust their quantity up or down to help the dog reach his healthy weight.

Often dogs will refuse to eat at first. This could be due to anxiety or depression associated with the transition, or it could be due to their personal preferences. Not everyone feeds dogs high quality kibble and foster dogs often come from situations where they have been eating table scraps or low quality food that is appetizing but basically junk food. Don't try different foods until you find one that is appetizing. Instead, offer the food at meal times and, if it is refused for twenty minutes, pick up the bowl. Offer it again at the next meal time. By the end of the second day, the dog should be eating the kibble.

If that sounds too heartless, you can try putting a topper on the kibble. I call this "priming the pump". If you put a teaspoon of high quality wet food on top of the kibble, the dog might start eating the wet food and just keep going until the bowl is empty. Similarly, sometimes the dog has low appetite due to an upper respiratory illness, like kennel cough. If the scent of the kibble is enhanced by a little tuna or parmesan cheese, the dog could become more interested in eating. Another caveat – some dogs just can't eat with a lot of distraction around them. You may need to move the food to a very quiet environment and sit quietly with him for twenty minutes until he feels safe enough to eat.

One way or another, it is important to have the foster dog eating on a regular schedule. By having a regular eating schedule, the dog will also have a regular potty schedule. Watch for him to need to go potty about an hour or two after meal time.

Case Study #6 Miguel and Claudia, - This is Miguel and Claudia's first time fostering as well. They have a lab mix named Luna who has happily accepted her foster sister, Penny, to the pack. Luna and Penny play together, walk together, snuggle up together, and eat separately. Luna loves her kibble, especially since Miguel likes to put a little bit of dinner scraps on top of the kibble at night. Luna would happily eat both her dinner and Penny's! But Penny isn't a fan of kibble. Miguel put a little chicken and rice on Penny's meal the first day and she carefully extracted every grain of rice from the kibble and left the rest.

For two and a half days Penny has refused the kibble, and Claudia is starting to worry that she isn't going to eat. "Let's just feed her chicken and rice! It's ok! I can cook extra for Penny, just so she will eat!" Claudia says. But Miguel knows. When a dog is hungry enough, she will eat. He sits with Penny in the living room, and her bowl of kibble with a little chicken and rice. He hands Penny the chicken from the bowl. Then he takes some kibble and offers it to her from his hand. "Come on, lovely, try it. It's good! You'll like it!" he says. Penny takes a kibble from his hand and rolls it around her mouth a bit. Then she crunches. Miguel praises Penny as he gives her a few more. When he puts down the bowl, Penny gradually eats the rest of the food. "Good girl, Penny, good girl. See? We're not trying to starve you here. But we're also not going to be your personal chefs. You've got this."

Sit on Command

Teaching your foster to sit is relatively easy and has high rewards. Imagine being in a foreign country and you've now learned the words for hotel (crate), bathroom (go potty) and you know how and when to get food. The sit command takes your foster one step further by teaching him to take a rest because you're going to be his tour guide. When you're out for a walk and you stop the dog to sit for a treat, it's as if you're saying "don't worry, I've got everything under control, even out here". The dog looks at your eyes as you look at theirs and you connect.

Before teaching sit, you'll want to teach the dog his name. Have several training treats in your pocket and say his name in a happy voice. When the dog looks you in the eye, give it a treat. If you need to, hold the treat up next to your eye to direct his gaze. Move around so that you break that gaze and the dog needs to move to look you in the eye again. Do this for five minutes at a time, a few times a day, and your foster will soon be coming to look you in the eye at the sound of his name.

Now that you have your foster's attention, and he knows that treats are coming, start to teach "sit". Call their name and get them to look at you. Now, take the treat and hold it towards the dog, and then slightly over his nose, and then back over his head, guiding his head up. As his nose follows the treat, his back end can either move backwards or move down. Reward him for baby steps - for following the treat, next time for leaning back, and a big bonus payout of treats if his back end goes into a sit. Practice this daily, in multiple locations, and you'll proudly be able to tell the new adopters how easy he is to train.

Walking Nicely on a Leash

Dogs who have been surrendered to a rescue come from a variety of situations. They may have been beloved pets who have already been through training classes and are well socialized. On the other hand, the dog may have lived relatively isolated, never taken anywhere in a car or on leash. Sometimes, the dog's first experience with a collar and a leash is when the rescue puts a collar on him at the shelter and walks him on leash to the transport vehicle. It is nice to acclimate the dog to the leash prior to his adoption so that the dog can walk with the new owners to their vehicle.

Now, I'm not talking about teaching the dog to heel on command and walk calmly next to you through the neighborhood pet supply store. I'm simply setting the goal of having the dog accept being leashed and walk in the same direction as you when you move. Puppies and adult dogs can become bucking broncos when a leash is attached to their collar. I've seen dogs freeze when we walk out the door just as often as I've seen them try to pull me down the block. We're looking to build the dog's confidence, as they learn that the person on the other end of the leash is walking with them. It's a relatively low bar, and it really helps to get the dog ready for his new life.

First off, all leash training should be accompanied by a lot of treats. Start off by checking that the dog's collar isn't too tight or too loose. You should be able to fit two fingers comfortably under the collar without there being a gap. Inside the house or yard, attach a standard leather or nylon four or six foot leash to the dog's collar and drop it on the ground. Give the dog lots of praise and treats as you walk around the house. Next, pick up the leash and walk backwards in front of the dog, saying his name, giving praise, and feeding him treats. Now that you're both walking in the same direction, walk around the house and yard a bit, giving intermittent treats. If the dog stops or pulls backwards, move towards the dog to loosen the lead. Try to keep some slack in the line, so that the dog does not feel the tension on his neck. Go through the indoor practice as many times as needed until you're confident that the dog will walk with you when you attach the leash.

If the dog is not fully vaccinated, is not healthy or if the rescue does not want the dog exposed to the neighborhood, do not risk going outside. Otherwise, take some treats and poop bags and continue practicing walking outside. Go slowly. Let the dog sniff things, explore things, and take treats. The purpose of this walk is not to get your exercise or to physically tire out the dog. The purpose is to acclimate the dog to the sights and sounds of outside while staying with you for reassurance and positive associations through treats. Don't set a goal of where you want to go. Set the goal for how long you want to be out. Then practice going up and down the same block, past the same houses, crossing the street together, and processing the world. Get your foster dog's attention frequently so that he looks you in the eye and associates you and the treats you're giving with this walking experience.

Now, this all sounds calm and happy, but what if you have a foster who wants to run wild and free and take your arm off with him? That sort of dog can see the straight line of the sidewalk as a runway at a drag race. Again, your goal isn't to get to the corner, your goal is to be outside walking calmly. There are a few training tricks to balance the dog's excited energy and to get him to recognize that you are there with him on this walk. One is the "u-turn" technique. This is, basically, making a u-turn every time he starts to pull. This creates some slack in the line, and a smart dog can figure out that he can't go the direction he wants to go unless the leash is loose. Another technique, which I really like, is the "crooked walk" technique. That is where you put a lot of twists and turns in the walk between here and the corner. For example, you might cross the street a few times, do a couple of u-turns, go around the street trees, walk up a few driveways, stop unexpectedly, and change your pace from fast to slow to fast again. The crooked walk keeps the dog guessing and keeps it paying attention to you. When he chooses to change direction and follow you, give praise and treats. Have fun with it. You'll find that there are a lot of fun obstacles that make the walk interesting.

Case study #6 - Continued. Miguel and Claudia have been doing so well with fostering Penny. But they have a secret. Their dog, Luna, is terrible on leash. She pulls. She barks. She tries to chase squirrels. To be honest, Miguel and Claudia don't walk Luna as much as they would like to because she gets so excited. Even though Luna and Penny do everything together, they have decided not to walk Luna and Penny together. They would not want Penny to learn bad behaviors from Luna. How embarrassing! But it's ok. They are now committed to working with both the dogs on walking nicely. Miguel and Claudia leash up the two dogs. It's chaotic with Luna jumping up and down and baking and Penny getting excited as well.

Claudia grabs her treat bag and poop bags and takes Penny out the backyard and to the gate. Once she's calm, they step out together. They head off to the right, Claudia praising Penny and giving her treats for giving her eye contact. Penny pulls ahead a bit when she sees a neighbor and falls behind a lot when she hears a loud truck, but she is generally confident enough to explore, sniff, and receive treats. Claudia and Penny do a slow walk down to the corner and turn around. That's when they see Miguel and Luna coming out the front door. Miguel has Luna sit and look him in the eyes before she is allowed to move forward and turn left.

"She's going to head down that sidewalk like a rocket." Claudia thinks to herself. But no, Miguel is not following Luna's usual routine. He has Luna get in the car and then get out again. They cross the street together, go around the light post, and then he has Luna go up on the low retaining wall for a sit. They go around a tree twice together, back across the street, around the fire hydrant, and up to the neighbor's porch. Anyone else watching would think

Miguel was lost or crazy, but not Claudia. All she sees is that Luna is following Miguel, anticipating the next u-turn, and more interested in treats than pulling. It's a good start!

Medical attention

One goal of rescue is to adopt out healthy dogs who will not contribute to the pet overpopulation crisis. As the foster, you will be responsible for medical care for your dog and for transportation to and from the veterinarian, as needed. As we discussed earlier, the rescue could provide transportation assistance, but you will be responsible for the hands-on care in your home.

So, what kind of medical attention is necessary? This really depends on the dog. For example, if you've agreed to foster a dog with mange then you would be responsible for medicating the dog with oral or topical prescriptions. Many dogs come from the shelter with kennel cough, an upper respiratory infection that is treated with medications, and need to be isolated from your own dogs to prevent transmission. Some will have diarrhea caused by intestinal worms, giardia, coccidia, a change in diet, stress, or, worst case scenario, parvovirus. You will want to look at the dog's poop after he goes so that you can see if it looks healthy. Treatment could be a single dewormer pill, or a series of daily pills.

Even if your rescue dog shows up on your doorstep as a healthy dog, the stress of transition and exposure to new things could result in a dog that becomes sick. If you notice signs of loose stools, cough, excessively watery eyes, excessive hair loss, vomiting, etc., notify the rescue coordinator immediately. Be ready to give them a description of your observation and a history of what the dog had to eat and where he has been. Be proactive when it comes to identifying and treating illnesses.

For dogs that are not spayed or neutered, the rescue will make an appointment for the surgery. They will be checking in with you regarding your availability to drop off and pick up your foster. They will give you pre-operative instructions regarding when the dog's last meal should be and what time to drop him off. After surgery, pain killers may be prescribed if needed and the dog may go home with a surgical cone (aka the cone of shame) around his neck. Follow the directions of the veterinarian explicitly unless the rescue coordinator says otherwise. Be prepared for the dog to seem disoriented, to the point of even whining and crying the first night. This is a typical response to the anesthesia, since they become quite confused as it wears off. In my experience, male dogs are feeling just fine the next day, but females take longer to recover. Your female foster might take a couple of days before she is her happy self again. After all, female spays are much more invasive and extensive than male neuters. At the end of the recovery period, you may need to return for suture removal, the sutures may dissolve, or suture glue might have been used. Review the medical documents which accompany the surgery to see if the dog needs to return for suture removal.

Besides the spay or neuter surgery, the other medical care which your foster will need are microchipping and vaccinations. The rescue will have a policy regarding which vaccinations the foster dogs receive, which type of microchip they administer, and where these procedures are done. Check in with the rescue coordinator to coordinate the vaccination and microchip administration.

Monitoring

You will, inevitably, know more about your foster dog than the main rescue coordinators will know. When the dog is in your home, you have the opportunity to monitor their health and behavior, and it is up to you to communicate these observations to the main rescue volunteers. For example, you might notice that your dog occasionally limps, drinks excessively, has a rash, or pees twenty times a day. Any of these things could be an indication of a medical need that needs short term or long-term care. You could notice that the dog prefers women over men, is cat obsessed, barks at everything, or has a lot of energy. These observations are also important, since they could help the rescue select the ideal adoptive home. Since you have constant contact with the foster dog, you are the one primarily responsible for monitoring his medical, social, and exercise requirements.

The table below shows a responsibility matrix related to responsibilities for care. This is just an example, based off of the rescues that I have encountered. The rescue you choose to volunteer for may have different expectations, but this table will give you some talking points so that expectations are understood on both sides.

CARING FOR YOUR FOSTER DOG

Care Responsibility Matrix Example		
Commitments	Rescue	Foster
Safety	Yes	Yes
Routine	No	Yes
Boundaries	No	Yes
Socialization	No	Yes
Crate training	No	Yes
Potty Training	No	Yes
Training to Sit	No	Yes
Walking on lead	No	Yes
Medical attention	Veterinary care	In-home care
Medical expenses	Yes	No
Transport to/from medical care	May arrange for transportation	May volunteer for transportation
Identifying new medical needs	Yes	Yes
Continuous monitoring	Only occasional	Yes

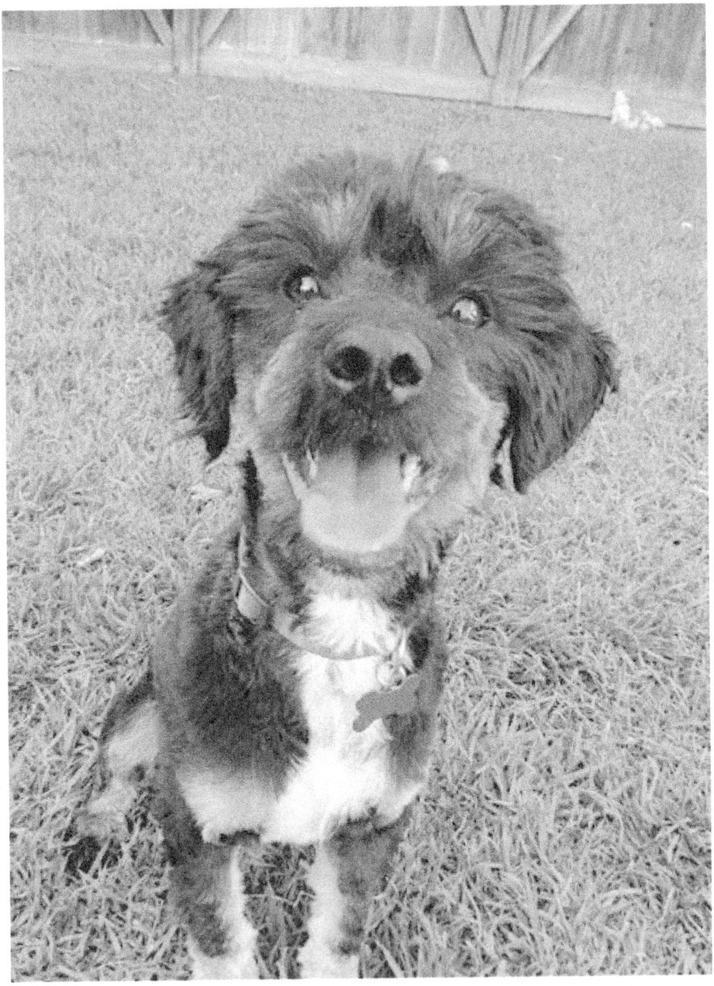

13

Adoption Time

When is my foster ready for adoption?

You've had your foster long enough to integrate them into your home, get them spayed or neutered, and accomplish a few training goals. Is the dog now ready for adoption? Well, that depends on the policy of the rescue. Some groups will post the dog for adoption as soon as all of the medical goals are accomplished. Other groups will want you to hold on to the dog for a couple of weeks, until his personality really blossoms and he is socially ready for the transition. Still others will wait until you know the dog well enough to make decisions on what the best fit will be. In any case, the dog will need to be medically and socially ready to make the transition into his forever home. For example, if you are fostering a dog for a city shelter, they will have medical and social goals to reach before you return the dog to the shelter. If you are fostering puppies, then they will need to be at least eight weeks old and have one round of vaccinations prior to adoption. Check in with the rescue coordinator and ask about their policy regarding when dogs are posted for adoption.

Posting for adoption

When a foster dog is ready for adoption, the rescue coordinator will write up a profile for the dog and, along with a few good photos, make a posting on the rescue's website, Petfinder.com, Adoptapet.com, and/or other websites. Since you know the dog the best, you should give the rescue coordinator information about the dog's exercise requirements, socialization, and personality. The best way to attract the right applicant is by accurately describing your foster dog. If you're a good writer, you can write up your own bio for your foster dog.

Case Study #7 - Myra. Myra has been fostering Ruby in her home as a new foster dog and wants potential adopters to know as much as possible about her prior to applying for her. She's a good dog, with a lot of love, who Myra has been treating as one of her own. She writes this bio and sends it to the rescue coordinator.

"Ruby is a three year old boxer-hound mix. She weighs 57 pounds, is potty trained, crate trained, up to date on shots, microchipped, spayed, and knows some basic obedience. Ruby was rescued just in time from the south-central L.A. shelter. Ruby was very thin and had obviously been left outside all the time by her last owners.

In foster care, Ruby has become a healthy, happy, loving dog who is very good with dogs and people of all ages and sizes. Ruby likes to go on walks around the park and for rides in the car. Like most boxers, she is friendly, eager to learn, energetic, a good jumper, and great with kids. Like most hounds she likes to watch birds and squirrels, watch and listen to the neighborhood kids outside, run with her tongue hanging out the side of her mouth and then nap on a soft bed in the house. Ruby isn't much of a barker and doesn't jump up on people. She likes training and is responding well to positive reinforcement (treats, and praise). An ideal owner would be one who is eager to take her to training class.

After all that time being an outside dog, we'd like to find Ruby a home where she could really be a part of the family. Ruby has a soft and gentle personality and would do well with kids as long as she was not accidentally let out front to run off. Her sweet personality is ready to find a family of her own who will show her all the joys of life that she missed out on. In foster care Ruby has really flourished with love and we'd like to see her continue on that path."

Myra sends the rescue coordinator photos for Ruby's ad which show her with dogs, lounging at home, and outside in the sun. She wants people to have the image in their mind of a beautiful boxer-hound mix who would fit in perfectly in their home.

Only a foster can capture moments of the dog in a home. It is up to you, as the foster, to take photos of your dog to which people will relate. The rescue coordinator might have photos of your foster at the shelter, in the transport vehicle, or, maybe at the coordinator's home. You can provide photos of your foster dog in the bath, playing frisbee, snoozing in the sun, with your cat, sitting nicely for a treat, or on walks. Those photos help people to realize what it would be like to live with your foster dog. Try to take some good photos and share them with the volunteer who assembles the bios.

Helping to find a home for your foster

If you're already taking photos of your foster, is it okay to post them on your social media? Check with your rescue coordinator and they will most likely say "yes, please!" Networking your foster can absolutely help them to find the right home more quickly. Use social media with hashtags associated with your rescue. Direct people to the website where they can apply to adopt the dog. Walk the dog in your neighborhood wearing a bandana that says "Adopt me!" Send out an email blast to friends so they know you have a foster dog in need of a home. When you're at the vet say "this is my foster dog" when you're talking to others in the waiting room.

If your rescue group has public adoption events, promote the event on social media and then attend the event. Being at the event to answer peoples' questions about your foster dog can help to screen out homes that aren't a good fit and get him into one that works out.

After a while, people will know you foster and will automatically go to you if they are looking to adopt a dog. Just be aware that you are not the person who approves adopters - that is the rescue's responsibility. Even if you think someone is perfect for your foster dog, they still need to go through the same process as anyone else. Never transfer a foster dog without the rescue group's prior permission. On the flip side, people will know that you foster and will try to get you to foster a dog in need. Again, remind them that they need to go through the rescue to inquire if the nonprofit organization will take responsibility for the dog and then have you foster it. You're part of a rescue team, so be aware of how your communications reflect on the group and, as a volunteer foster, do not make commitments on behalf of the rescue organization.

The adoption process

When a dog is ready for adoption, the rescue's main focus is to make a good match between the dog and the new owner(s). The goal is to find a home that will keep the dog safe and healthy, meet all of his physical and emotional needs, provide the dog with appropriate boundaries and training, and provide a stable home for the rest of his life. This may seem like a high bar but, except for the "rest of his life" phrase, you have been meeting all of those goals as the foster parent. Just like the nonprofit rescue got to know and trust you, they strive to get to know and trust the adopter in a short period of time.

The first step in most adoptions is the application. This is a standard form that an interested party fills out to indicate that they would like to adopt a particular dog. Organizations will have their own individual forms, but they all follow a certain pattern.

1. Identity and contact information- The top of the form will ask for the name, home address, contact information, if they own or rent, and if the landlord is ok with their

addition of a dog to their household. The purpose of these questions is to have the means to contact the potential adopter and to make sure that they have considered their rental agreement up front.

2. <u>Description of the household</u> - These questions will ask how many people live in the home, their ages, who will be primarily responsible, how many other pets are in the home, the ages of the children, etc. It may also ask the number of hours the dog will be left alone, where the dog will sleep, and if all household members are in agreement on adopting a dog. One purpose of these questions is to see if adopters meet the rescue's minimum age requirement for adoption Another is to see if there are any incompatibilities with this particular dog. For example, if a dog is considered to be unsafe for very young children, then the rescue could deny the application if the family has a toddler. Or, if the minimum age requirement to adopt is 18, then a 14 year old adopter filling out the form might be required to have their parent apply instead.

3. <u>Previous dog experience</u> - These questions could range from asking the adopter to describe their history with dogs as pets or could ask if they have breed-specific experience. Questions could also cover previous training classes, how they plan to train this dog, or how they would react if the dog chewed up a favorite shoe. The purpose here is to gauge the person's ability to take on the new challenge of adopting this particular dog. Someone who has never had a dog before might not understand that a Belgian malinois will need a lot of time and attention or that a dachshund will have issues with a house with three flights of stairs. The rescue needs to try to match the dog's needs with the

applicant who is most likely able to fulfill those needs.

4. <u>Keeping the dog safe and healthy</u> - These questions might ask if the current pets are spayed/neutered and up to date on shots, if the back yard is fully fenced, who their current veterinarian is, what their veterinary care limit is, if they have a pool, what the upper financial limit for veterinary care will be, or if they use flea prevention treatments. They may ask if the potential adopter will accommodate a home safety check from a volunteer. Each of these is designed to assess the safety of the home and the medical care that will be available to the dog.

5. <u>Long-term care</u> - These questions will center around long-term plans. For example, what would the applicant do if they needed to move out of state, if the dog needs extensive medical care in old age or if there are any circumstances in which they would not keep the dog. Since the rescue's goal is to place the dog in one home for the rest of his life, these questions are on the application to see if the adopter has the same goal.

6. <u>Other questions</u> - There may be other types of questions, each with the goal of learning about the adopter so that the right dog-person match can be made. They could range from asking if the person is very active (in case the dog has high exercise needs), if their resident dog can come to meet the dog prior to adoption, or why they want to adopt a dog. As much as these questions are designed to get to know the potential adopter, they are also designed to inspire the adopter to think about the responsibilities that come with adopting a dog.

After receiving an application, the rescue coordinator will decide if this home qualifies to adopt a dog from the rescue group. The standards may vary from group to group and from one dog to another, but the general requirements will be the same - they are looking for a home to provide the dog with safety, stability, medical care, training, socialization, boundaries, exercise, love, kindness, compassion, and a forever home with their family.

During the screening process, the rescue will typically reach out to a potential adopter over the phone (or in person, at an adoption event) to discuss their application. Some groups will ask the foster to have this phone screening conversation. In either case, the rescue group and the foster will discuss the application together and come to an agreement before approving the adopter. The foster's input during the screening phase can be critical to the success of the adoption, since the foster best knows the dog's daily needs. The exceptions are, of course, fostering for a shelter or humane society where the dog is returned to the shelter when they are ready to be adopted and adoption events where the foster is not in attendance.

Case Study #7 - Continued. About a week after Ruby's ad is posted, the rescue coordinator reaches out to Myra with an approved application for review. The potential adopters are a family in town - a dad who is a firefighter, a stay at home mom, and twin boys, age 12. The application states that they do not have a dog, but previously had a bloodhound who passed away at Christmastime. They are looking for a dog to be a companion for the kids and also help protect the house when dad is away at the station. They have their own home and would take the dog with them if they ever moved away. When they go on vacation, they plan to kennel Ruby at the vet's office or have a friend take care of her. Ruby would sleep inside in a crate at night. They have taken their previous dogs to training and feel comfortable training Ruby themselves.

As a follow-up Myra asks the adoption coordinator about the statement that Ruby would be for protection. She's not really a protection dog. The adoption coordinator specifies that Ruby would be an inside-outside dog, and they want a dog with a loud bark who would deter intruders or door-to-door salesmen. "Well, no problem there! She has a bark on her! Those guys selling solar just left pamphlets and walked on!" Myra says. But what about the training? Could they take Ruby to training, she wonders. The adoption coordinator says that she asked them about that, too, and that the mom wants to work on training with the boys involved. Apparently they have been watching a couple of YouTube influencers who post videos about using clicker training for teaching tricks. Learning about the family, Myra feels that they're a pretty good fit for Ruby. She gives the rescue coordinator some times which would work well for a meet and greet.

14

The Meet and Greet

<u>Adoption events</u>

For many people, once their application is approved, the first time they meet the dog is at the meet and greet. Some rescues use adoption events to introduce approved adopters to meet their potential pet. If your foster dog is scheduled to meet an adopter at an event, prepare the dog and prepare your household. Either arrange for transportation or transport your foster dog to the event. Take with you and medical paperwork which you might have, such as a certificate of sterility and records of vaccinations. Also take with you a small bag that has two to four days' worth of the kibble the dog has been eating to give to the adopter. This will help them to transition the dog from this food to their preferred food without stomach upset. Brush the dog a bit before you show up so that he looks adoption ready.

Preparing your household means letting them know that your foster dog most likely will not be coming back from the event.

THE MEET AND GREET

Goodbyes aren't necessarily happy, but emphasize that this is a happy day for your foster dog. The dog has, in a way, "graduated" from rescue. Acknowledge any feelings that people have, including feeling the loss. Thank people (and pets!) for being such a great foster team. Tell the foster dog that you've enjoyed having him at your house and that you are pretty sure you've found his forever home.

When you show up at the event, let the coordinators know you are there, and ask where you and the dog should go. It will likely be a little hectic with multiple dogs in the area. Wait at a comfortable distance until the event coordinator lets you know where your foster dog should go. Make sure it is ok for you to stay for the meet and greet, since some events have limited space. When the new adopters arrive, the event coordinator will be responsible for any paperwork, transfer of medical documents, and communication of the rescue group's policies. Your contribution will be to answer any questions the adapter has about the dog's needs, personality, and health. Be sure to congratulate the adopters on the addition of their new family member, since this is an exciting day for them. When you say your goodbyes, be positive. Elaborate displays of affection towards the dog or expressing stress over their parting can worry the dog. Make sure your foster gets the impression that this is a normal and favorable transition in their life, not something of concern.

Home adoptions

Many groups perform adoptions right at the foster's home. In this scenario, you, as the foster, are responsible for the process from start to finish. It is similar to a mini adoption event, tailored to your foster and their new family. If you are not comfortable meeting strangers in your home, talk with the rescue coordinator about alternatives. There may be a rescue coordinator's home, rescue facility, or a quiet park where the potential adopters can meet you and the dog. A successful "home adoption" can take place in your home or at another designated location.

For the home adoption, the rescue will coordinate a good time for you to have the potential adopter over to your home for a meet and greet. Set aside at least an hour in your schedule. The assumption is that the adopter is coming to meet the dog and, if it's a good fit, they will take the dog home with them that day. However, some rescues will require additional steps, such as a home check, prior to the dog's release to the new home. Check with the rescue coordinator to make sure you understand the intent of the meet and greet and the steps involved in the adoption process. Compile the medical records, 2-4 days worth of the dog's food, and any other adoption paperwork (such as adoption contracts) given to you by the rescue.

Prior to the arrival of the adoption applicant, set the scene for the meeting. Put other dogs in a different room or outside. Have some treats and favorite toys available. This will create a calm environment for them to get to know your foster and reward him for meeting them. If you are meeting at a place outside your home, take the dog there early so that he can sniff around and get used to the sights and sounds of the location.

As with the adoption events, you will also need to prepare your household for the meet and greet. Small children, in particular, might not understand that the dog will be leaving with the new people. I like to emphasize that we have been looking for the dog's family and you believe you've found them. That the people coming over are the dog's people and they are very excited to meet him and take him home and love him forever. Acknowledge any sad feelings, since this can feel like a loss, and thank them for being such a good foster to a dog who really needed it.

In our family, it's typically my husband who has the hardest time letting go. Since I have been the one screening the adoption applications, he doesn't necessarily know anything about the new family except that they are taking away his pal. I always let him know all of the wonderful things about the people coming over to adopt. For example, our last foster was a rambunctious terrier who chased chickens and, so, was relegated to living outdoors in a locked cage. The couple coming to adopt him had lost their young terrier the previous summer due to bloat (a traumatic physical issue). They had a nice house in a good neighborhood where the dog would have a good yard, sleep in the bedroom, be taken for walks in a big park nearby, and get lots of training. Letting him remember what the dog's life used to be like and understand what the dog's new life would entail made the transition a bit easier for us both.

To prepare myself for the adoption, I have a conversation with the dog. I imagine it could help him, too. It might go something like this:

"Max, do you remember when you came to stay with us a few

weeks ago? Remember how I explained to you that you would be staying with us until we found your new family? Well, I think we found them and they would like to meet you today. There's a dad and a kid and I told them all about you - how you love to play fetch and snuggle on the couch and eat jerky. This family will always keep you safe, to make sure you get good food every day, to teach you new things, have fun together, give you tennis balls, and always love you. I think this is it, Max. When they come over, get to know them and, if it's okay with everyone, you'll go home with them to live forever. Thank you for being such a good dog here in our home. I have enjoyed getting to know you and helping you to find this new family."

Now that you've prepared yourself, your foster dog, and your household for the adoption, it's time for the meet and greet. In some cases, people will bring their own dog to the meet and greet to make sure it is a good match. In these cases, let people know that they should leave their dog in the car (on cool days) or outside with a family member for 5-10 minutes until the dog has met the people first. This stepwise approach brings down the energy in the room.

With the dog waiting in another room or behind a baby gate, have the family come inside the house and sit down. Then let the dog in and calmly sit down as well. Bringing everyone to a seated position on the furniture or on the floor makes for a less intimidating situation for the dog.

Your foster will likely gravitate to the people he knows (you and your household) at first. As he goes to explore the newcomers, praise him for saying hello. Some dogs will be too shy to go up to new people. In this case, make sure that the potential adopters are the ones who have the treats to hand out or drop casually near them. You should not baby or pet the dog, which rewards him for hanging back with you. Instead, all of the treats and pets should be from the guests. New people should never force the dog to sit with them, be touched by them, or take treats from their hand.

If, after 5-10 minutes of casually talking about the foster while waiting for him to warm up to them, the dog still isn't approaching them, one thing I like to do is bring out one of my own dogs. I know my dogs will go right up to any guest, seeking attention and treats. When my foster sees that his friend is getting rewards for accepting new people, he's more likely to try it himself. Another thing I'll try with shy dogs is having the guest play with their favorite squeaky toy. Some dogs can't think about treats when they are stressed but can think about the fact that someone has that toy squeaking. A third trick is to take the group out to the back yard. Now, instead of having two or four people staring at the dog, they are in motion in an open space. This gives the dog the chance to come up from behind the person and sniff them. Sometimes all that is needed to break the ice is a little more room and a couple of toys to throw around on the lawn. Before long the dog might be going up to the potential adopter to ask them to throw the ball again.

If the potential adopters have their dog with them, then there are a few ways to introduce the dogs. First, you can go for a walk together. Leash up your foster dog and have someone walk the other dog at a bit of a distance. Distance could be a block away, across the street, or 15 feet ahead of you. Watch your foster for signs of stress, such as walking stiffly, barking, or raised hairs on the back of the neck. If things are fine, gradually close the gap while giving praise and allowing your foster to sniff the other dog's scent in the environment. After a while, the two dogs will be sniffing each other while walking together. If this has gone well, then take them back home and let them get to know each other off leash.

Another way to let the two dogs meet is by using a fully fenced location, such as your yard or an empty dog park. While keeping your foster dog inside, let the new dog into your yard through a gate. Keep both dogs' leashes on, but let them drag the leashes on the ground behind them. Don't guide them. The guest dog might be quite excited about the new environment sniffing and marking the perimeter. Wait for the guest dog to relax a bit and for your dog to relax as they watch the dog out a window. If both

THE MEET AND GREET

dogs seem calm and interested, then let the foster dog out into the yard. Hopefully they will meet each other with a friendly demeanor. If so, then take off the leashes and let them interact socially. However, not all meetings go as planned. Be prepared to step on or grab the leashes if a fight breaks out.

For any dog-dog meeting, the most important thing is keeping both dogs safe. You may not know that your foster will react in an aggressive way to the new dog. Check in with your foster coordinator prior to introducing an adopter's dog to your foster for further guidance on how to best avoid or handle issues.

Once everyone has met each other, and you've given the potential adopters time to ask all of their questions, the potential adopters need to decide if they want to complete the adoption. Offer them some alone time to talk together about the decision. If they need to go home to discuss and arrange another time to come back, that is ok. Never rush people to make a decision about a lifetime commitment. Nine times out of ten, when I have an approved applicant come to my house for a meet and greet, they are prepared to take the dog home unless there is some sort of glaring red flag. One out of ten times, people need time to talk together to make sure the household is on the same page or they decide to go home and think about it. It is unusual to hear back that they have decided not to adopt this dog at this time, but it is not out of the question. Always thank people for considering a rescue dog.

Most likely, you are the only person to meet this potential adopter in person. The rescue coordinator has seen the application and has spoken with them on the phone, but you have had the opportunity to get to know them even better. Sometimes people say things at the meet and greet which they wouldn't have said otherwise. For example, I've had children give information that is the opposite of what the adult put on the application. If you have serious reservations about their honesty, ability to properly care for your foster, or their commitment to the life of the dog, step aside and call the rescue coordinator. You can politely let the potential know that you don't think it is a good fit. A more direct approach would be to let them know that you need to have further approval from the rescue group and that, if they agree to the adoption moving forward, you will arrange for them to come back another day. You are the face of the rescue, so use tact and kindness when saying goodbye.

Let's say it's a great match all around. The potential adopters are excited, you're excited, the dog is excited - it's a good day for all. What comes next? Your rescue organization will likely have paperwork for the adopter to sign, transferring the responsibility of the dog to the new owner. Some groups do the final paperwork after a trial period (1-2 weeks in the new home). The new adopter should also receive copies of medical paperwork and instructions on how to contact the rescue if there are any issues. The adoption fee should be collected, by check, cash, or electronic payment method such as Venmo or Zelle.

Finally, take an adoption photo of the new family with their new dog. This photo can, with their permission, be used on social media. The adoption photo should be forwarded to the new family to capture this significant event in their life. Leash up the dog and congratulate everyone as they walk out the door. If your foster hesitates to go with them, then you can assist them in loading the dog into the car. I have to say, most of my fosters don't even look back. They happily walk out and start their new life.

Here is a checklist to help you remember the tasks to cover during a meet and greet in your home.

1. Set the scene
2. Prepare your household
3. Prepare your foster pet and yourself
4. Meet the new adopters
5. Introduce the dog to the adopters
6. Introduce the adopters' dog to the foster dog (if applicable)
7. Answer all of their questions about the foster dog

8. Give them a moment alone to decide if they will adopt today
9. Decide if there are any major red flags that should be addressed – call the rescue & stop adoption today
10. Agree that this is a good match and move forward with finalization
11. Go over medical paperwork with adopter
12. Go over microchip paperwork, pointing out how to register the microchip
13. Give them a small amount of the dog's food
14. Take a photo of the dog with the family
15. Leash up the dog
16. Congratulate the new adopters!
17. Say your goodbyes and send them on their way

Case Study #8 - Karen. - It is just about Christmas - December 22nd, and Karen is expecting approved adopters to come meet one of the three puppies she is fostering. She knows it will be a little hectic, since she has three puppies (12 weeks old), her own two dogs, her toddler, her mother, her wife, and a teenage cousin all living in the house. She lets everyone know that the first of the adopters is scheduled to come by this evening. "You're really taking my puppies away from me?" her wife joked around. "I'm going to miss the midnight potty trips and the whining at dawn!"

Karen knows that the sarcasm was just a mask for a bit of sadness. The puppies have been there for about three weeks, and it has taken everyone to help potty train and socialize them. Everyone is so attached to the little pitbull mix puppies. Today is the first bittersweet adoption day of three that they have planned.

In preparation, Karen checks to make sure that the paperwork for the right puppy is on the table. She has a little bag of puppy kibble for the adopters along with an information packet and goodie bag which the rescue gives to all adopters. About ten minutes before the scheduled time, there is a ring at the door. A nice couple in their mid-fifties is anxiously waiting. Karen welcomes them into the house, and has them take a seat in the living room. The adopters can see that all three pups are in the kitchen behind a baby gate. When Karen lets them in, they run right for the couple, showering them with puppy kisses. Right away the couple gravitates towards the little black pup with the white blaze on his forehead. "This is Miko, right? He's even cuter than the pictures!" the older gentleman says.

Over the next half hour, Karen tells the couple everything that *they need to know about Miko – how he's been the most eager at mealtimes, has a love for the hedgehog stuffie, and he loves to wrestle his smaller sister but he always loses. They go over the paperwork, and talk about when the next round of shots is due and how to pay the adoption fee.*

The couple is eager to take Miko home. They have brought a new collar and tag for him, with his new name "Magic", and their phone number listed. The photo that Karen takes of the three of them is classic – two people looking at the camera and one puppy in their laps, trying to chew on someone's ear. As the couple carries Miko (now Magic) to the car, Karen calls out to them "Congratulations on your new family member! Thank you for adopting!"

15

After the Adoption

After the adoption is complete, call or text the rescue coordinator to let them know that the dog has gone to his new home. Let your family and your pets know that everything went well and that they did a fabulous job of getting the foster dog adoption ready. It's a great day for all involved. Celebrate! Here is one more dog who came from a shelter, the streets, neglect, homelessness, or another short-term situation who has found a loving owner who will take care of him for the rest of his life.

So, if it's a great day, why do you feel so conflicted? I often do. I've been fostering for over ten years and I still cry a bit sometimes after my foster gets adopted. It is a bittersweet moment. The objective has been achieved, the dog is happy, and the adopters are happy. The time you spent training, socializing, and caring for the dog have all set him up for success. Your foster went from a smelly, unneutered, outside dog who was afraid of the sprinklers to a handsome, confident, family dog who is ready to take on the world. You have done a good job at loving this dog as if he was one of your own.

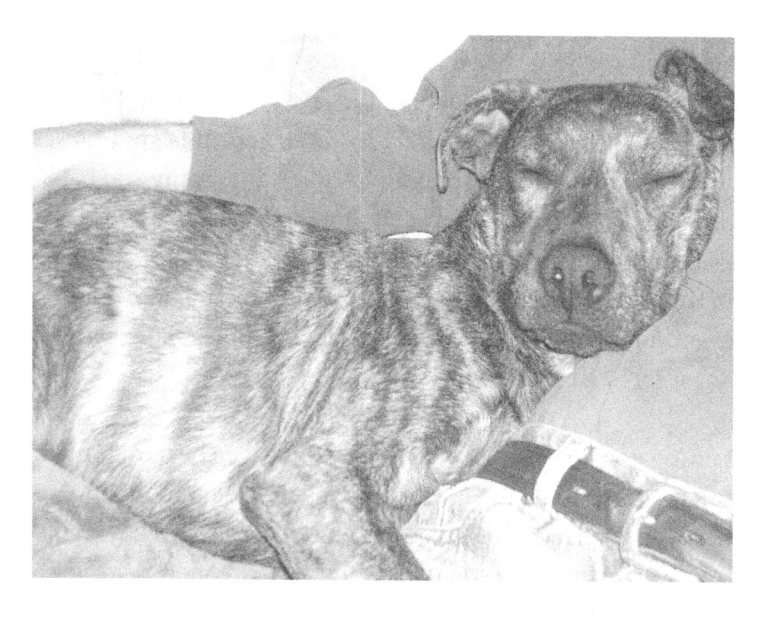

Over the weeks or months you fostered the dog, you built a bond of love and trust and friendship. Now your house feels a little too empty and lifeless. It's ok to be a little sad with the loss of that friendship. Will you ever see your foster again? In all likeliness, probably not. You may get an occasional update from the adopter (which is such a treat!) and there may even be an opportunity to become friends with the adopters if they are interested. But, from today onward, the responsibility for and joy of loving that dog is theirs.

A lot of people say that they couldn't possibly foster because it would be too hard to give them up. I say that the joy of helping them outweighs the difficulty of seeing them go. It is far better to help that dog in need and feel a little sad when they leave than it is to do nothing. Fostering isn't all joy and puppies. It's accidents on your carpet, dug up flowers, coaxing a dog past scary sidewalk grates, regimented feeding times, and having that guest choose to gravitate towards your husband rather than to you. It's lots of hoping for the right family and being disappointed by applicants who want to give the dog as a gift or use him for security purposes out in the yard or give up the dog in three years after grad school. It's volunteering for adoption events on a Sunday and coming home three hours later without any interested parties. It's hard.

Letting go of them at the end of their stay can be hard for you. But from the point of view of that dog, it's been life changing. It's been good food every day, a friend who teaches them things, treats, structure, and snuggles. For your foster dog, being with you has meant being able to get out of a bad situation, never whelp another litter of puppies, relax, and let down their guard to trust. It has been a true joy from your foster dog's viewpoint, with even more joy to come in the future. You have helped to change that dog's life in a profound way.

They say that true charity is thankless, so I know that you are not doing this for the praise, but thank you. Thank you for choosing to do what is hard so that this foster dog and hopefully the next and the next and the next will all benefit from your kindness. Thank you for seeing a way in which you can help and for stepping up to volunteer. Thank you for taking on the challenges and persevering. From me and my pack, thank you for choosing to foster a rescue dog.

Case Study #8 – Continued Miko and his two siblings have all been adopted. The third of the puppies has gone, and Karen is cleaning up all things puppy related. "Man, they were so messy!" she says out loud. Her wife hears her from the other room and calls back "They were such a pain! All the potty accidents and spilled kibble and sharp little teeth. So why do I miss them so much?"

The whole house feels a little down and also more calm. The chaos of the foster puppies is over, but so is the enjoyment of them. The house is just so .... Quiet. Karen never wanted a puppy again, let alone three, but here she was missing the puppies. She'll probably never see what they look like all grown up, what they'll act like, how they'll do in obedience classes, what silly Halloween costumes their owners might put on them. She's given them a good start in life, but she knows she won't see them grow up to be good ambassadors for the bully breed.

At dinnertime, the household gets together to talk about how fun it was to foster three puppies and all of the emotions that they are feeling now that they are gone. Karen's mom loved the little girl puppy, and was so happy that such a perfect home came along. Karen's wife commented on how Miko's parents seemed like the kinds of people who really understood dogs. They discussed how these three puppies had been abandoned in a dumpster like trash. But look at them now! They all have families who treasure them! It couldn't have happened if they hadn't stepped up to help. Karen raises her glass and says "Here's to the pups! May they never know a hard day again!"

AFTER THE ADOPTION

When a Dog is Returned

Sometimes you think it's over, but it's not really over. Occasionally, the adoption just doesn't work out. The adopter may not have really been ready for a new dog, the dog may have exhibited new behaviors in the new home. Someone in the home might be surprisingly allergic. Maybe you and the person who helped to screen the application just didn't see something which indicated that this was not the right home. For whatever reason, it just wasn't a good fit. You might feel guilty, disappointed, or sad, but it's not your fault. You did your best, the rescue did their best, the dog did his best, and it just didn't work out. That's ok. No one can predict exactly how things will go. I've seen dogs returned within two days and I've also seen people reach out to the rescue years later asking them to take the dog back.

It doesn't matter what happened, what matters is that the rescue organization acts as a safety net for the dog, so that he will never be in a shelter again. Logistically, the new owner should first contact the rescue (not the foster) to return the dog. If you have the room and if you are willing to take the dog back, then you can offer to foster him again. You are under no obligation to take him back into your home - the rescue will find another foster if, for whatever reason, you cannot take him back. The rescue will find the dog another home with a loving family who does their best to give him a lifetime of love and care.

16

Other Ways to Volunteer

What if you've come this far and you have decided that you can't foster after all? Through this process, you may have realized that a long-term or short-term foster assignment will require more time, money, or energy than you have at this time. Don't feel bad. There are many other ways in which you can volunteer to help dogs which do not involve taking one home. Here are just some of the examples.

1. <u>Volunteer at your local shelter</u>. Many animal shelters have volunteer programs. Programs may include bathing shelter dogs, greeting the public, showing dogs to potential adopters, helping at mobile events, assisting kennel staff, assisting in the onsite clinic, photographing shelter pets, exercising shelter pets, and doing community education. By volunteering at the shelter, you can help improve the quality of life for dogs in need, improve their chances of getting adopted, and advocate for spaying/neutering of pets.

2. Donate supplies or do fundraising. The care of foster dogs can be quite pricey and every non-profit rescue organization can use the donation of supplies and funds. You could, for example, organize a neighborhood food drive for a particular rescue and ask neighbors to donate bags of food. Many organizations have active Amazon Wishlists (I listed one example in the appendix). Wishlists allow you to see the exact type and number of each item the rescue needs and the supplies will ship directly to the rescue headquarters. Several of my friends choose to raise funds for rescues in lieu of birthday gifts. Facebook fundraisers are an easy way to raise money for the nonprofit you select.
3. Transportation. Several people choose to volunteer to do animal transport, which is always appreciated by any rescue. This can be as simple as picking up a dog and dropping him off at the veterinarian for care, or it could be as complex as helping to fly multiple dogs from one state to another. Volunteers have been responsible for helping to move dogs from counties with high rates of pet overpopulation to rescues with people waiting to adopt. Sometimes the only hurdle in getting a dog into a fabulous foster home is having a transporter available at the right time. If you have a car and a little free time, consider contacting rescues and offering help transporting as needed.
4. Dog sitting or dog walking. When a foster goes on vacation, the rescue scrambles to find a temporary foster home for the dog. This can be difficult for the dog and for the foster coordinator. Volunteers can help alleviate the stress by dog sitting for a weekend or more as needed. You can also volunteer to help out fosters by offering to do mid-day or

evening walks with a dog who has high exercise needs.
5. <u>Training.</u> From time to time the biggest thing standing in the way of a dog getting adopted is their lack of training. In this case, a rescue might opt to look into training classes for the dog. A volunteer who has previous training could sign up to take the dog to weekly training or work with the dog in his foster home. Even without training experience, by taking a dog to class you can help him/her to learn as you learn as well.
6. <u>Adoption events.</u> Some groups hold adoption events on weekends. The volunteers for the events are not necessarily the dogs' foster parents. Event volunteers greet the public, handout information, care for the dogs, and help on-site adoptions go smoothly. By volunteering at events, you have the opportunity to share in the joy of a new owner connecting with and taking home a dog in need.
7. <u>Website design and maintenance.</u> People who run dog rescues aren't always web savvy. If you know how to design a website, then why not offer to make a website for a group who doesn't have one? Or to update the information for them? This would reduce the overall operating costs while helping with marketing. Another similar way in which you could help is in maintaining the Petfinder or Adoptapet account. Every time there is a new dog listed, their profile needs to be made and submitted. Profiles need to be removed when dogs get adopted. Taking this task off of someone's hands can free up their time and expedite adoptions.
8. <u>Record keeping.</u> Are you good with organization and numbers? Can you compile data in spreadsheets? Can you help build a better system for tracking expenses? Can you

do taxes? Every 501c3 nonprofit is responsible for keeping updated financial records, reporting finances at quarterly meetings, and filing taxes. If you have a knack for record keeping, and you have time to volunteer, you could be a godsend to a rescue in need. Oftentimes the record keeping is done by the same person who is fielding calls about dogs who need help and calls from potential adopters. If you can help with record keeping, then dogs can be saved and adopted out more quickly.

9. Social Media Networking. Besides using their website and pet adoption websites, rescues rely on social media to get the word out about adoptable dogs. Are you good at taking great photos of dogs? Why not volunteer to take photos of dogs who need more promotion? Are you an Instagram aficionado? Why not offer to run the group's Instagram? Are you more of a Facebooker? You could offer to moderate the group's Facebook. Do you have social media accounts? You could help to get dogs adopted by sharing their information on your own social media accounts. The better the photos of a dog, the more exposure they have, the higher chance there is of them getting adopted. You can also help by posting a link to this book, so more people will know how to foster a rescue dog!

10. Education and outreach There are fewer shelter dogs for each person who chooses to adopt instead of shopping. For every person who chooses not to casually breed their dog, a litter of homeless puppies gets adopted. Are you educated about pet overpopulation, shelter statistics, and the advantage of adopting a dog in need? Are you someone people come to for advice? Then you're already helping. Keep getting the word out. You are part of the solution.

11. <u>Volunteer vacation.</u> Why not use some vacation time to help dogs in need? Several organizations around the world have programs where you can actively volunteer while staying on site at the rescue. One of the best programs in the United States is at Best Friends Animal Society in Kenab, Utah. There you can help out by doing feedings, cleaning kennels, walking dogs, making toys, and playing with dogs. You can even take a dog back to your cabin for a sleepover.

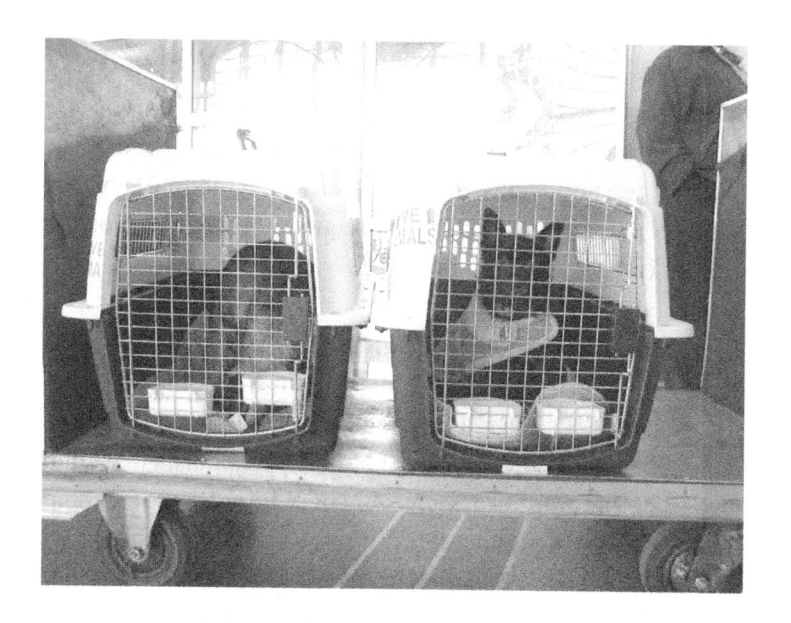

17

Frequently Asked Questions (FAQ's)

Things don't always go as planned. When you are fostering a dog for a rescue you can be surprised by the rescue policies, by health scares, or by animal behavior. Here are some of my answers to frequently asked questions in various categories.

Q: Where do the dogs come from?

A: It depends. If you're fostering for a local shelter, then the dogs are from the shelter. They have been relinquished by their owners or they were strays whose owners did not come for them. If you're fostering for a nonprofit rescue group, then the dogs may come from the shelter. Many shelter programs have rescue coordinators who reach out to rescue groups to try to alleviate the shelter. Rescue groups often qualify for shelter programs whereby they can take the dogs into their system for a reduced fee. Some rescue dogs come from the community. People reach out to dog rescues when they cannot keep their dog for various reasons.

I fostered one lovely corgi named Fender. His owners desperately relinquished him to rescue because he bit a child in their home and they did not want him around children anymore. We learned that the twelve year old boy had been teasing the dog. He was picking him up around the middle in a rough way when he was bitten. Upon examination at the veterinarian's office, it was discovered that Fender had a large tumor in his spleen that was nearly ready to burst. Fender received medical care and was placed into an adults-only home for the rest of his life.

Sometimes dogs are not relinquished, but are lost. When someone in the local community reaches out to a rescue because they have found a lost dog, most rescues will not take in the dog unless the person has already tried to find the original owners. It is generally the policy of rescues that the person who finds a dog must comply with local shelter policies, i.e. take the dog to the shelter or alert the shelter so that they can help find the original owner. If a dog already has a home, then a good rescue organization will want to see that dog returned to its owners. Only after attempts have been exhausted will a rescue take a found dog from the shelter system..

Q: I live in an apartment. Do I need to own a home with a yard to foster?

A: Not at all! If you can provide a safe and stable home and take the dog out for potty breaks,and your apartment allows dogs, then you can foster a dog. There are some lovely apartments that have grassy areas designated for dogs. When you contact a rescue, make sure to specify that you live in an apartment and that your apartment allows dogs. Provide the apartment manager's phone number so that they can double check that the complex is dog friendly.

Q: I saw the sweetest senior dog who needs a foster. Should I foster him, knowing that it might take longer for him to get adopted?

I love senior dogs. They are typically mellow, loving, trained, low energy and appreciate a good warm bed. Seniors can be the easiest dogs to foster. I have a good friend who has fostered multiple senior dogs and, although they might require more medical attention, what she gets in return is priceless. She knows that the dogs in her care truly need her love and care. There are rescue groups that specialize in senior dogs and some which specialize in hospice cases. It is heartbreaking to see senior dogs in the shelter, so confused and wondering where their family went. Sometimes a senior citizen passes away and leaves behind a senior dog. The examples of senior dogs in need are endless. If you feel called to foster a senior dog, your gift to the community and to that dog will be greatly appreciated.

Q: I really want to adopt my foster dog. No really. I'm in love. I can't stand the thought of letting him go. Can I adopt him?

If you have thought long and hard about it and you want to add your foster dog to your family, then, by all means, please do. Sometimes the heart wants what it wants. I have a friend who loves her demure German shepherd. She took the lead in fostering, eventually bringing in a large goofy malamute. Her husband fell in love with the dog. The wife was certain that this was just another foster, since he chewed on things, shed profusely, and was generally much too silly. But her husband kept hounding her that his malamute couldn't go. When the friend reached out to her friends in rescue, we had the resounding response, "let the man have his dog!" It was so obvious to us, as outsiders, that this was a love match and that the malamute had found his forever home. The dog matured, was easily trained, and became a lifelong friend to the man who wanted him. No regrets.

Q: My wife and I thought we were ready for fostering, but this dog is making us fight more. The dog is driving us crazy. Can we send it back?

The short answer is yes. Rescue organizations are responsible for taking back the dog if it is not a good fit for your home. Sometimes the foster dog is just too much for us - too energetic, too needy, too difficult to train, too aggressive, too shy, too much work, too stressful for our other dog, too cat obsessed, too anything. But that's ok. It's not always a good fit.

The long answer is yes, but give it some time first. The first three days, while a dog is decompressing, can be very stressful. I had one chihuahua who was so afraid of her new home that she crawled up into the recliner to hide. There was another foster who was absolutely convinced that the kittens which were closed up in the guest bedroom were vermin in need of extinction. I've done dog-dog introductions too quickly and was sure that my dog would never accept the strange new dog. Ask the rescue coordinator for advice, read up a bit on dog training, work together as a couple, and you can get through the initial hurdles. If you're still overwhelmed, concerned about safety, or have other reasons for sending the dog back, then use your safety net and ask the rescue to take back the dog. Hopefully a different dog will be a better fit.

Q: My foster dog bit me. Should I tell the rescue coordinator, or would that give him a bad rap? Will my foster still be adoptable or will they euthanize him?

Always tell the rescue coordinator if the dog bit you and breaks skin. How the group treats dog bites will depend on the group's policy. Tell them as much as you can recall about the circumstances so that they can assess the gravity of the situation. The dog may be unadoptable, or it may be adoptable under certain circumstances - such as only to homes without children or only to an owner who has experience managing a dog who bites. In any case, it is a liability that the rescue needs to assess and decide the right path forward.

Q: My foster dog growls at my other dog when he's eating. It's a bit scary. Is he dangerous? What should I do?

Growling aggressively around highly valuable items (food, treats, toys) is known as resource guarding. To start, feed your dog and the foster dog in separate rooms. After they are finished eating, pick up the bowls and let them interact again. Do not risk a dog fight or a human bite. Do not leave treats, such as bones or raw hides, out in the open for him to potentially guard as well. Next, talk with your rescue coordinator and ask for advice on reducing resource guarding. There are several dog training websites and books dedicated to resource guarding, so check a few out. It is usually quite manageable.

FREQUENTLY ASKED QUESTIONS (FAQ'S)

Q: I don't love my foster dog. I barely like him, really. Am I a bad foster parent?

No, not at all. You don't have to love them all, you just have to take care of them until their owner comes along. Just because you find your foster dog to be stinky and of low intelligence compared with other dogs, that does not make you a bad foster parent. You're a gem for having him as your houseguest.

Q: How much should I feed this dog?

It depends. Bags of dog food sometimes have guidelines on them, but they are just guidelines. There are also some online calculators. I recommend starting with a published guideline and measuring the food for each meal using a measuring cup. Watch the dog's weight. If he starts to gain weight, then reduce the food by ¼ or ⅛ cup. I had a foster dog who was so fat that his neck was as wide as his head. By measuring his food I was able to gradually get him down to a healthy weight. You have to consistently know how much you're feeding him to be able to adjust his weight up or down.

Q: My foster dog is so afraid of me that it runs and hides. How do I get him to trust me?

This is another topic which could be a whole book. Here are some techniques which have helped me.

1. Keep a drag lead on the dog. A drag lead is a leash that is only a few feet long and has no loop at the end. You can step on the leash to stop the dog, use the leash gently to

lead the dog where it needs to go, or to keep the dog from going out the door. Once the dog stops running, you can take off the drag lead.
2. Keep really good treats in your pocket. Don't expect him to come up to you for a treat. Either drop treats near him or toss them to him. Gradually drop the treats nearer and nearer to you. Make positive associations with your voice by giving treats while you talk with him.
3. Use crate training to acclimate him to his surroundings. By putting him in the crate which is located in a busy part of your room, he can start to acclimate to the sights and sounds of the household.
4. Don't ever risk a dog bite. Don't reach under furniture with your hand to get the dog out. If you really need to pick up the dog, use a towel or blanket. Toss the towel over his head and body. Make sure his eyes and mouth are under the towel before you reach towards him to move him physically. If he is small, you can wrap him up like a burrito while picking him up. By using a towel, the dog can get more used to your touch without being directly touched.

Q: My foster dog has diarrhea, both inside and out of the house. Will it resolve or should I get some medical help?

It's hard to know. A change in diet can cause diarrhea for a dog with a sensitive stomach, as can the stress of being in a new situation. Giardia, coccidia, worms, and parvo can also cause diarrhea - and parvo is deadly. Let the rescue coordinator know that the dog has loose stools and ask about getting treatment.

FREQUENTLY ASKED QUESTIONS (FAQ'S)

It is best not to wait for more than twenty-four hours to seek a solution.

Q: Will someone want this dog? I'm concerned because he's not pretty / hyper / has potty accidents / sheds a lot.

There is a lid for every pot. What you find attractive / desirable / entertaining is not the same as what others like. I had a foster dog who refused to go potty outside when it rained and it drove me crazy. Their new owner did not care one bit. They already had a dog who was, apparently, made of sugar and they put down potty pads whenever it was needed. There was another foster dog who was so high energy that I could not tire him out. He was always looking for something to get into and could walk for miles a day without tiring. He was adopted by someone who had previously had the same breed of terrier who loved him at first sight. Everyone has their deal breakers and their must-haves and they will not be the same as yours.

Q: The rescue has not posted my dog for adoption yet, and it's been a while. How do I get them to move the process along?

Not all rescue groups are as responsive as you would like them to be. Do what you can to help them with the process. Take really good pictures and send them along. Write up a short paragraph about the dog so they can use that for the posting. Network the dog through your facebook or through email, with the instructions that interested people can contact the rescue. Ask the adoption coordinator if you can help with Petfinder or website postings. The squeaky wheel gets the grease. You might have to call or text the adoption coordinator multiple times to get a response. Also, you can ask if you can have your email address included in the posting, so that people can contact you directly. See if you can help to pre-screen potential adopters. If the rescue is too busy to post dogs, then they might be too busy to answer inquiries to adopt.

Q: The rescue organization is being unresponsive to my calls and emails. I think I'm stuck with this foster dog. Help!

If you do not feel supported by the rescue organization, it is not a good fit. There are many other rescue groups who would return your calls, answer your questions, post the dog for adoption, and not leave you hanging like this. Please consider fostering for another organization.

As for the dog who has been left in your care? Contact the rescue organization again, through email and over the phone, with the express request to return the dog. Let them know that you wish to return him by a certain date. On that date, if they still have not reached out to you, message them again, reminding them of your request to return the dog by this date. After that, you can let them know that you are no longer fostering for the organization. Next, reach out to other local rescues and ask if they can help you. They may be able to help you post and place the dog in an ad, separate from the original posting. If the rescue who abandoned you gets upset, you will hear from them and you can then return the dog. Overall, it's a tricky situation and I hope you get it resolved in a way that does not deter you from fostering again.

Q: I need to go on vacation. Do I need to find a dog sitter for my foster dog?

When you have vacation plans, make sure you tell the adoption coordinator that you will be unavailable. Give as much advance notice as possible. Ask them if someone else can watch your foster dog. If the rescue does not provide you with an option, you may need to find a dog sitter or boarding situation for while you are on vacation.

Q: The rescue organization is pressuring me to take a second foster dog. I hate to hear about other dogs who might be euthanized and I do have the space, but I'm not sure if I can take on more work right now. How do I say no?

A good rescue organization will respect your boundaries. They are highly motivated to take in more dogs because they get calls and emails from shelters all the time. There are so many dogs on the euthanasia list that it is heartbreaking. It is the responsibility of the rescue coordinators to take those calls and to shield the fosters from the stress that they feel. I've known quite a few fosters who have gotten burned out because they take on more than they can sustainably do. They have rescue coordinators telling them the sad stories of how, if they don't take this litter of puppies, they will all die. Nobody wants to be responsible for puppies dying, so volunteer fosters take on more dogs. Pretty soon they feel overwhelmed, like the weight of the world is on their shoulders and their whole home is a kennel.

You cannot save them all. That is part of the sadness of dog rescue. But you can focus on them, one at a time, and then take the next one when there is space. If you can foster on at a time for the next three or five or ten years, then that is better than taking in nine dogs all at once and deciding you can't do it.

Only you can decide what you are willing and able to give. You are not a bad person for saying no. Having boundaries will keep you fostering for longer.

Q: My dog needs emergency medical attention. Where do I go? Will the rescue pay for it?

A: The rescue should have provided you with information on the nearest emergency vet. If not, and it is really an emergency, then go immediately. Call the rescue coordinator on your way there. They may prefer to have you go to a different nearby location. Have the coordinator on the phone when you arrive so that they can talk directly to the staff at the vet office. The rescue will want their name on the dog's emergency records and should pay with a credit card over the phone. If not, then you'll need to decide if you are willing to pay for the emergency care without knowing if you will be reimbursed until after the fact.

Q: My dog hates the rescue dog. They have gotten into fights, but nobody has been hurt. Do I wait it out, separate them, or send the dog back? I hate to think that I've failed.

You have not failed. Sometimes it's just not a good fit. Contact the rescue coordinator and discuss the fighting behavior and the surrounding circumstances. You will likely need to separate the two dogs when you are not actively supervising them, at the least. Sometimes our dogs just don't get along with all dogs just like we do not get along with all people. One of my dogs is dog selective. He is a bit of the "fun police", barking at dogs who are squirrely. The other dog accepts anyone who has four legs. They are individuals, just like humans.

Q: I have a co-worker who really wants to adopt my foster dog. Can I adopt him to her?

Only the dog rescue organization can approve an adopter. Your co-worker will need to go through the same process that other people go through. Give your co-worker the information for the rescue. Let her know the steps to the adoption process - application, screening, approval, meet and greet, etc. You can guide her through the process but you cannot guarantee that she will be selected to adopt the dog. The rescue coordinator may already have applications that they are reviewing, and they may have a first-come-first-served policy. The rescue may choose the best applicant out of a pool of applications. Encourage your co-worker to adopt but do not promise that she will get priority.

Q: I'm having a birthday party for my kid. Is it ok for everyone to meet my foster dog?

Large gatherings can be very stressful for dogs. Even mellow dogs can feel trapped or manhandled by a group of children. Also, if, for example, you're fostering a puppy who is not fully vaccinated, then germs tracked in by many pairs of little shoes can get the puppy sick. It is best not to take these chances with your foster dog. Keep him safely closed away in another room until the kids leave.

Q: My foster dog got out of the house and I can't find him! Help!

Hopefully you're reading this before an emergency, not during. Immediately go out looking for your foster dog while also contacting the rescue coordinator. Enlist everyone from your household and take treats and a leash with you. The rescue coordinator may help you look and should be on alert for any incoming calls (since the rescue's number is on the tag). If you see the dog, do not chase him or yell at him. Many foster dogs used to be stray dogs and will run if approached. It can be helpful to have multiple people help corral the dog into a smaller and safer area, such as a back yard or parking lot. Very calmly approach the dog while tossing treats. Take your time gaining his trust with treats and a happy voice. When you're close enough to pet the dog, then gently hold the collar while you are petting him. Attach the leash and take him home.

If it takes longer to find the dog, make flyers with his photo and the rescue's information on it. Pass the flyers out to neighbors in the vicinity and post them in public places. Keep an eye on the local shelter website, in case animal control picks him up as a stray. Above all, enlist the rescue's help in finding him. Although you may feel bad and embarrassed, put the dog's safety first by enlisting others to help you.

Q: I found a dog on the streets. Can I foster it and find it a home?

The purpose of rescue is to help homeless dogs find their forever homes. If you have found a dog, you are obligated to help him get back to his owners, not find new owners. Even if you are convinced that you can find the dog a better home, you need to think about the dog's current owners and how sad they must be. The dog may have an elderly owner who needs him for company or a kid at home who is posting flyers.

First, if it is safe for you, then you can bring the dog home to keep him safe. If there is a dog tag, call the number and let the owner know that you have the dog safely in your home. Arrange for a time for them to pick up their dog. If there is no dog tag, then put a collar and leash on the dog. Head over to the nearest veterinary office to have them scan the dog for a microchip. If the dog is microchipped, then the microchip company can help put you in touch with the owners.

If the dog has no form of identification, then make flyers and post them in public locations. Make postings on social media, such as Facebook, Nextdoor, and Craigslist, searching for the owner. Finally, contact the animal shelter. They will likely advise you to bring the dog to the shelter so they can add him to their found pets listing. The animal shelter is the most public way for someone to find their lost dog.

If no-one comes for the dog, then you can adopt him from the shelter and help find him a new home. Hopefully you will have the support of a local rescue group who will help you with posting him on line, screening potential adopters, and placing him in a good home.

Q: My foster dog has stitches but he also really needs a bath. How can I spruce him up without risking an infection?

When a dog has stitches, you should not submerge them in water because of the risk of infection. You can use a wet washcloth to rub some of the surface dirt off of his coat. There are also dry shampoos for dogs which will leave him smelling and looking a whole lot better until he's ready for a real bath.

Q: My foster dog has the longest nails - it looks painful. But he won't let me touch his feet. How do I trim his nails?

If it is a medical issue, then contact the rescue coordinator and ask them to make an appointment at their vet or groomer for a nail trimming. Sometimes dogs have been so neglected that they need nail trims, baths, grooming, or to be shaved down. Take note of and communicate any grooming needs which you cannot perform.

Q: Why is the adoption fee so high? The rescue has hardly spent any money on my foster dog.

Each rescue will set their adoption fee according to what they think is fair, what people are comfortable paying, and what will keep the rescue afloat. There are basic medical costs, such as the cost of vaccinations, flea treatment, deworming, microchip, and spay or neuter. Then there are the costs of supplies, gas, and shelter fees. Some rescue organizations will rent and run their own kennel. The biggest expenses to a rescue, however, are the medical fees (expected or unexpected) for the dogs who need extra care to be healthy. This could range from setting a broken leg to luxating patella surgery to removing a badly damaged eye which cannot be saved. Veterinary care can cost in the thousands. Besides fundraising, rescues can recoup those veterinary expenses by charging a little more for healthy dogs.

For example, getting a puppy ready for adoption might cost $300, but the rescue could charge a $400 adoption fee. The extra $100 can go towards covering the dental work that a senior dog needs.

If you think that your rescue charges unfairly for adoptions, then you may want to ask them about their policy and/or inquire about fostering for a different organization. You can also choose to check the public documents and the tax exempt status of the rescue group using the IRS website.

Q: Do my foster dog's toys, food, and supplies also go with him when he gets adopted?

Supplies which you and the organization purchased belong to you and the organization. They do not belong to the dog. The collar with the identification tag will typically go with him, so that there is contact information in case he is lost before a new tag is purchased. You should send a small portion of his food with him so that the new owners can gradually transition him to a new food. If there is a toy you purchased which he is particularly fond of, you can send it along with him. You will need the crate, bed, and other supplies for your next foster dog.

Q: I don't have copies of my foster dog's medical records. How do we do the meet and greet without medical paperwork?

Always check to see that the medical records are complete and ready prior to having someone meet the foster dog. You can do the meet and greet, but you should not transfer the dog without the medical records. Check with the adoption coordinator to see if you can get a copy of the medical paperwork for the potential adopters before they arrive.

Q: People came over to meet my foster dog, but they're not sure if they want to adopt him or not. How do I convince them that he is a really good dog?

Adopting a dog is a lifetime commitment. Potential adopters should think hard about their desire to adopt a dog. If the people need more time to think about it, do not pressure them to decide on the spot. It needs to be a good mutual fit.

That said, sometimes dogs just don't show well. And sometimes people expect an instant love connection. I've had several dogs who didn't really want to interact with the adopters (or their dog) when they came for the meet and greet. Dogs can be quite shy around strangers or around new dogs. Make sure to remind them that your foster took time to warm up to you and will take time to warm up to them. He has been through a lot in a short amount of time, and this is another big transition for him. Remind them of all the strides that he's made so far – from the day you got him to today – and that he has even more potential for growth ahead of him. Don't try to sell them on him, but put things into perspective for them.

Q: My foster dog is so attached to me. Will he be okay when he goes to his new home?

I've had many dogs become very attached to me, and I see that as a good thing. Here is this dog who was in a shelter environment, who has transitioned to living in home where he's been trained, neutered, and acclimated. The dog has done all of that in a short amount of time and has also bonded with me. If he can do that, that means that he will do it again, in his new home. The fact that he bonded with me quickly means that he will bond with his new owner quickly.

Don't worry that he'll feel abandoned by you. Know for certain that he will feel the desire for a strong bond with his new owner.

Q: My foster dog is OBSESSED with the cat. I'm afraid for the cat. How do I get him to just calm down?

Some dogs have a very high prey drive. They still have that primal part of their brain that wants to hunt and kill. Keep your cat away from the dog, for the cat's safety. If possible, set up a separate room for the cat and have her stay there until the foster dog is adopted. Teach the dog the "leave it" command for when he obsesses at the door to the cat's room. If, after a few days or a week the dog still seems obsessed, you may want to ask the foster coordinator for a different dog.

18

References and Resources

https://www.animalhumanesociety.org/volunteer/become-foster-volunteer

https://www.petfinder.com/animal-shelters-and-rescues/fostering-dogs/before-you-foster/

https://be.chewy.com/want-to-foster-an-animal-heres-everything-you-need-to-know/

https://www.akc.org/akc-rescue-network/

https://azhuskyrescue.com/

www.petfinder.com

www.adoptapet.me

https://www.soonergoldenrescue.org/

REFERENCES AND RESOURCES

https://amazingdogs.org/why-foster/

www.chewy.com

https://www.amazon.com/hz/wishlist/ls/8WZMGM11XFGI?ref_=wl_share&fbclid=IwAR3-nTV4vj7uCdvMKSFnKyMm7znajX5_ET5wei1AaqrbOZgJabpDOjodO1M

https://www.rocketdogrescue.org/volunteer-2/volunteer-opportunities/

http://orangecountyanimalservicesfl.net/GetInvolved/Volunteer.aspx

List of toxic plants: https://www.aspca.org/pet-care/animal-poison-control/dogs-plant-list

List of dog toxins https://www.petmd.com/dog/poisoning/poisons-dogs

Kong toys website https://www.kongcompany.com/

Compostable dog bags: https://earthrated.com/

Earth Bath dog shampoo: https://www.earthbath.com/collections/dogs

Martingale collar: 8 Best Martingale Dog Collars [2023 Reviews] (k9ofmine.com)

Crate Training: https://dogsbestlife.com/dog-training/crate-

training-your-dog/?cn-reloaded=1
https://www.thedodo.com/dodowell/crate-training-older-dog

Healthy dog treats: https://raleighncvet.com/nutrition-weight-management/11-healthy-natural-treats-for-dogs-in-your-kitchen/

Training treats: https://www.dailypaws.com/gear-apparel/training-products/best-dog-training-treats-according-to-trainer

Homemade dog treats: https://www.akc.org/expert-advice/lifestyle/homemade-dog-treats-recipes-tips/

US Nonprofit tax exempt status search:https://apps.irs.gov/app/eos/details/

What to do if you find a lost dog: https://www.americanhumane.org/fact-sheet/if-you-find-a-lost-pet/

Volunteer vacations: https://www.volunteerhq.org/volunteer-abroad-projects/wildlife-and-animal-care/?mkwid=s-dc_pcrid__pkw_animal%20volunteer%20vacation_pmt_p_&pgrid=1231453249188230&ptaid=kwd-76966048855434:loc-4084&msclkid=e98fc9d97f2f17636ce7adc5ee9f9410&utm_source=bing&utm_medium=cpc&utm_campaign=S%20%7C%20USA%20-%20Projects%20-%20High&utm_term=animal%20volunteer%20vacation&utm_content=USA%20-%20Animals%20-%20Volunteer%20Abroad

REFERENCES AND RESOURCES

Best Friends Animal Society: https://bestfriends.org/volunteer/animal-areas

Epilogue

If you have enjoyed this book, please help me to get this information out to others as well. Adding a review on Amazon.com will help to boost the book in the ratings. More visibility means more people considering fostering

You can also post a link to the book on your rescue organization's website. There is a paperback, a low-priced kindle book and the audiobook will be released this year.

If you run a 501(c)3 dog rescue, I will gladly send you a pdf copy of this book if you think it will help you. You can reach out to me at wblanda114@gmail.com for your copy. I plan on writing other books on topics related to rescue, and, as rescuers, I'd welcome your feedback for future projects.

My goal is to give people the tools they need so that there is an increase the number of people who volunteer to foster. In doing this, we can decrease the number of dogs who get euthanized every year. Please encourage others to do what they can to help out, pass along this book, and let's get some more dogs placed in forever homes.

Afterword

Ok, so the case studies were of fictional dogs and people, but who doesn't like a little closure? Where are they now?

Case Study #1 - Angela. Angela and her two roommates made a great fostering team. Their first foster, Marcus, was adopted by a nice family who had a standard poodle named Ken. Marcus and Ken became fast friends, with Ken the tall quiet type and Marcus the feisty protector of poodles. Angela and her roommates fostered four more dogs that year before Angela moved to New York City. After she moved, she couldn't foster anymore due to building restrictions, but she has always found ways to spread the word about dog rescue. Once she found a litter of abandoned kittens behind her cafe and she immediately reached out to a kitten rescue for help. Lately she's been seen taking peanuts to the Central Park squirrels.

Case Study #2 - Rachel. Where Rachel gets her strength from, nobody knows. Her first dog, Rocky, was adopted after nine months in her care. By then the senior yorkie, Mimi, had passed away already. Rachel knew that Mimi was just there for hospice care, but it still hit her hard. The second hospice care dog wasn't as difficult for her, though, or the third. Rachel's love for senior dogs is so strong that she helps them pass the rainbow bridge peacefully.

The fourth hospice care chihuahua mix ended up not being as old or as sick Thurman seemed to go backwards in age - becoming less continent, more playful, and utterly sassy with age. With good food, rest, and medical care, Thurman was nearly puppy-like again. He lived another six years as Rachel's hospice care dog, bringing life and love to the whole household.

Ten years into rescue, Rachel now takes on a bit less. She has one dog of her own, a cat, and fosters one senior dog at a time. She is a wealth of knowledge when it comes to all sorts of special foods and medical treatments.

Case Study #3 - Lawrence. He should have known. He really should have known. To put the punchline first, Lawrence was a foster failure.

When the gentleman from the golden retriever rescue brought over his big fluffy six year old foster boy named Bo, it was game over. From day one Lacey and Bo were fast friends, playing fetch together and wrestling like worms. Their silly antics made it hard to see giving up Bo. Put that together with his two teenage boys begging him to keep the big fluff, and Lawrence caved. Was it the boys' plan all along? Who knows. But we do know that Lawrence does not have one ounce of regret that Bo found them and has come to stay.

Case Study #4 - Earl. Hank and Mochi started off playing with each others' paws under the door and eventually ended up chasing each other down the halls during playtime. Earl would throw Mochi's mouse toys down the hall and it was a race to see who would get to it first. Sometimes Mochi would hide halfway

AFTERWORD

down the hall and swat at Hank as he ran by. Earl had never seen such a funny friendship between a cat and a dog.

Hank ended up being adopted by someone who had a corgi-pomeranian mix dog. They drove about an hour and a half to come get Hank, then visited with Earl for another hour and a half during the meet and greet. They promised to send Earl update photos of Hank as he got fit and trim.

After Hank, Earl fostered a couple of other dogs for the corgi rescue, but it was always hit or miss as to whether they would be cat friendly. They weren't all like Hank. Sometimes he felt bad for Mochi, like when one foster dog pushed over the gate, ate all of Mochi's food, and then dove into her litter box for "dessert".

Dogs can be so gross! What did Earl do? He reached out to a local cat and kitten rescue and offered to foster some kittens. Mochi has been quite a good foster sister to the rescue kittens and Earl's place has had a lot less fur to vacuum up.

Case Study #5 - Yan and Andrew. Bubba, their rottweiler mix foster, turned out to be a rather easy guest. He and Willow played nicely, tiring each other out, and then took up the whole sofa relaxing. After about a month, the shelter called, saying that they had a great applicant for Bubba and they would like Yan and Andrew to bring him back for a meet and greet. When they dropped Bubba off at the shelter, they said their goodbyes, hopeful that the adopter would love him. They waited and waited for the call to hear what happened. At the end of the day, Andrew called the shelter and learned that Bubba had been adopted.

Not knowing anything about Bubba's adopter was hard on Yan. There was a bit of closure missing, and she cried over the loss. She decided that she just couldn't foster anymore. However, a week later, the shelter's foster coordinator called, asking them to take in another dog. Andrew clearly explained that the way the adoption happened upset Yan, and they were not going to foster again. Apparently, there had been a miscommunication, though. The coordinator clarified that many people do not want to spend the extra time to be at the adoption event but that they are welcome to participate.. It would actually be very helpful if they had the time to be there!

After some consideration, Yan and Adrew decided to foster again. They even encouraged other people to volunteer at the shelter.

Case Study #6 - Miguel and Claudia. Luna, their lab, and Penny, their foster lab mix, got along from day one. By the time Penny was adopted three months later, she knew how to sit, lie down, come, and go into her crate on command. Penny's new owner was a young man in his late twenties who loves to hike and camp. Although Miguel and Claudia missed Penny (as did Luna!), they were content that the right home had come along for her.

Training Penny inspired Miguel to take Luna to some advanced training classes. They even tried out some agility! Claudia and Miguel continued to foster lab mixes, and each time they got a little bit better at learning which training techniques to use with which dog. Recently, Luna and Miguel passed the AKC Canine Good Citizen test. Afterwards, they celebrated with some homemade treats.

AFTERWORD

<u>Case Study #7 - Myra</u>. Ruby the boxer mix was not adopted by that family (firefighter dad, stay at home mom, two boys who are 12). Myra did everything right at the meet and greet, but Ruby just wasn't the right fit for the family. During the meeting at Myra's house, the boys were a bit rambunctious, wrestling with Ruby on the floor. Ruby got so excited that she tore one boy's shirt and then started barking at the two of them quite loudly. The family was concerned that Ruby could be aggressive, so they decided that they wanted to keep looking.

Myra was really disappointed that the adoption didn't go better. Maybe it was something she did? Ruby was a very good girl! After the family left, Myra called the rescue organization's adoption coordinator. They went step by step over what happened. It sounded like Ruby was just overstimulated. She didn't bite the boy, she pulled at his sleeve. And the barking was loud, but extremely playful. Too playful! What Myra could have done differently was to monitor the boys a bit more closely, stopping the wrestling when it got rough. It's okay to have boundaries, even with potential adopters!

Ruby ended up getting adopted a couple of weeks later by a very similar family. This time, though, the kids knew a lot more about interacting with dogs. They even signed Ruby up for obedience class, which she passed with flying colors.

<u>Case Study #8 - Karen</u>. Together with her family, Karen has heard the call of the puppies. They can't resist. About two to four times a year for the last four years, they have fostered as many as seven puppies. The seven puppies were from one pregnant mama dog who gave birth at their house. They thought

that it would be four or five dogs in a week or so, but it turned out to be seven the day after they got her.

It's been exhausting at times, but also a lot of fun. The rescue they volunteer for has been very supportive and also lets Karen help screen the potential adopters. Some of the puppies have gone to people who they know, so they've been able to see them grow up. The best part is that they have done this together and grown as a family - Karen, her wife, their daughter, Karen's mom, and even the stray family member who comes to stay from time to time.

If you have enjoyed this book, please help me to get this information out to others as well. Adding a review on Amazon.com will help to boost the book in the ratings. More visibility means more people considering fostering

You can also post a link to the book on your rescue organization's website. There is a paperback, a low-priced kindle book and the audiobook will be released this year.

If you run a 501(c)3 dog rescue, I will gladly send you a pdf copy of this book if you think it will help you. You can reach out to me at wblanda114@gmail.com for your copy. I plan on writing other books on topics related to rescue, and, as rescuers, I'd welcome your feedback for future projects.

My goal is to give people the tools they need so that there is an increase the number of people who volunteer to foster. In doing this, we can decrease the number of dogs who get euthanized every year. Please encourage others to do what they can to help out, pass along this book, and let's get some more dogs placed in forever homes.

Made in the USA
Monee, IL
28 January 2024